D0981869

WE ARE THE
CHAMPIONS

Transcontinental Books
1100 René-Lévesque Boulevard West
24th floor
Montreal (Quebec) H3B 4X9
Tel.: 514 340-3587
Toll-free 1-866-800-2500
www.livres.transcontinental.ca

**Bibliothèque et Archives nationales du Québec and Library and
Archives Canada cataloguing in publication**

Main entry under title:
We are the champions: the greatest hockey teams of all-time
At head of title: The hockey news.

ISBN 978-0-9813938-2-7

1. Hockey teams. 2. Hockey - History - 20th century. 3. National Hockey League. I. Fraser,
Edward, 1978- . II. Hockey news (Montréal, Québec).

GV847.W4 2010   796.962'64   C2010-941198-6

Project editor: Edward Fraser
Proofreader: Ronnie Shuker
Art director: Annick Desormeaux
Cover design: Jamie Hodgson
Photo editor: Erika Vanderveer

Printed in Canada
© Transcontinental Books, 2010
Legal deposit — 3rd quarter 2010
National Library of Quebec
National Library of Canada

We acknowledge the financial support of the Government of Canada through the Canada
Book Fund for our publishing activities and the Government of Quebec through the SODEC
Tax Credit for our publishing activities.

For information on special rates for corporate libraries and wholesale purchases, please
call 1-866-800-2500.

The Hockey News

Edited by Edward Fraser

WE ARE THE CHAMPIONS

THE GREATEST HOCKEY TEAMS OF ALL-TIME

Transcontinental Books

FOR SLOANE, MOM AND DAD

TABLE OF CONTENTS

We start with the best of the best the NHL has ever had to offer based upon longevity, chemistry, individual skill and domination against relative competition. Not every Cup winner makes the grade, but every one of the Top 25 is a champion.

Standout collections aren't the sole domain of the world's best league. In this section we explore teams that will be remembered for the ages, that came together on the international, minor pro and junior stages, leaving fans with memories for a lifetime.

Some NHL teams have multiple championships while others are still searching for their first glorious moment, but every organization has one that stands above the rest as the best of all-time. We detail the top dog from each of the current 30 squads.

INTRODUCTION

You hold history in your hands. As you leaf through the following pages, you'll find the squads that will forever be remembered as one of the best, a measuring stick for all future greats based either on their dynasties or short-term domination.

The bulk of the book is made up of our Top 25 NHL teams. Stacking up squads from different eras was a fascinating, yet prickly endeavor. How can you really compare collections from the Original Six years against those built under the oppression of the salary cap? Or what about those dynasties? How much stock should go towards an organization's maintenance of longevity? And what exactly makes a great team? Is it individual talent or a collective effort? There's only one factor that wasn't up for debate. As Alex Ovechkin simply, but brilliantly stated early in his career: "Cups is Cups." No championship, no consideration.

In the end, we looked at all of the above angles and more, and arrived at a list we feel represents a fair ranking based on how that team performed and excelled against the competition of its time. We don't expect you to agree, of course. As with any subjective list, the truth lies only in the mind of its creator. We do, however, hope you'll enjoy the debate it creates and the accompanying stories, which not only provide nuts-and-bolts recaps, but also unique tales and intimate views via the individuals who played on or were close to the teams themselves.

(A final note about the Top 25: We chose only one season from each dynasty or club that won multiple Cups in a short period of time. This was done in order to avoid repetition and, quite frankly, to prevent this work from reading like a biography of the Montreal Canadiens, who could easily occupy 15 of the spots without this proviso.)

The second part of the book examines the crème de la crème of the international scene and the minor pro and junior leagues. Much like the Top 25, the stories jump from decade to decade and provide wonderful anecdotes and information with names both familiar and unfamiliar popping up throughout.

In the third section, some of the lesser-lights take the stage as we focus on current NHL franchises and select the best bunch they've ever iced. We omitted team's seasons that were very closely tied to one of our greatest of all-time, but that wasn't an issue for several teams as "the best" was really a relative term (we're looking at you, Atlanta and Columbus).

Putting together this book was a labor of love and we hope we've shed some new light on these awe-inspiring tales. In the end, though, the kudos go to you for having the passion for this great sport and for taking the time to remember and reflect upon The Greatest Hockey Teams of All-Time. Enjoy.

Edward Fraser
Managing Editor
The Hockey News

TOP 25 NHL TEAMS OF ALL-TIME

No. 1

1976-77 MONTREAL CANADIENS

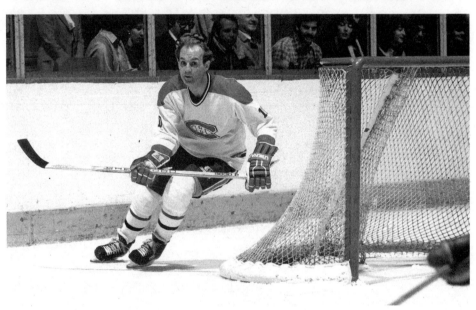

With his long locks always flowing behind him, Guy Lafleur won the Stanley Cup five times in Montreal and was named a first team all-star on six occasions.

IT MIGHT BE DIFFICULT TO BELIEVE, but the Montreal Canadiens actually had a losing record against the Boston Bruins in 1976-77. After one of those losses superstar Guy Lafleur said, "I will never accept losing. Never. The law of averages is bound to catch up with us, but that's no excuse for a bad performance."

And, that, in a nutshell, is what made the '76-77 Canadiens the greatest collection of talent in the history of the game. The rest of the NHL provided Montreal such feeble competition that they had to fabricate it from within by challenging themselves to be better and more dominating with every game. Practices, for the most part, were even more demanding than the games.

"When we scrimmaged, you were playing against the best players in the world," recalled Peter Mahovlich, who lost his spot on the first line to Jacques Lemaire that season, despite posting a team-record 82 assists the year before. "You couldn't help but get better because we had a bunch of guys who loved to be on the ice. Guy Lafleur loved to be on the ice. Steve Shutt loved to be on the ice. Larry Robinson loved to be on the ice and going at top speed. It was fun."

The Canadiens opened that season with a 10-1 win over the Pittsburgh Penguins, finished it with a 2-1 overtime win over the Boston Bruins in Game 4 of the Stanley Cup final and in between, they were the most electrifying, dominant and unstoppable team the NHL has ever seen. All told, they established 21 NHL records that season, including a 132-point performance that still stands as the league's benchmark. Their goal differential of 216 is by far the best in NHL history, 40 ahead of the next-best mark, which was established by the Habs the following season.

"EVEN THOUGH WE WERE WINNING ALL THE TIME, EVEN IF YOU HAD BUMPS AND BRUISES, YOU KEPT PLAYING BECAUSE YOU WERE SCARED TO DEATH OF LOSING YOUR SPOT IN THE LINEUP."
– PETER MAHOVLICH

They had nine players in the lineup who ultimately made their way to the Hockey Hall of Fame, along with coach Scotty Bowman and GM Sam Pollock. They became one of only two post-expansion teams (the 1970-71 Bruins were the other) to place four players – goalie Ken Dryden, defenseman Robinson, right winger Lafleur and left winger Shutt – on the first all-star team. The league might as well have held its awards ceremony at the Canadiens team banquet, since Lafleur won the Art Ross, Hart and Conn Smythe Trophies, Dryden and Michel Larocque the Vezina, Robinson the Norris and Bowman the Adams.

Had the Rocket Richard Trophy been in existence, Shutt would have taken it on the strength of a 60-goal season that established a record for left wingers. The Selke Trophy was established the next season, when Bob Gainey won his first of four consecutive honors as the league's best defensive forward.

When you consider Montreal's dominance that season, you must look at it through the prism of a four-year run in which the Habs won four Stanley Cups and established themselves as arguably the most dominant dynasty in the history of the sport. In those four years, the Canadiens lost just 46 games. To put the Canadiens' 60-8-12 record in 1976-77 into perspective, they're the only team in NHL history to play more than 60 games in a season and lose fewer than 10. In fact, prior to Montreal losing just 11 games the season before, the low-water mark for losses in a 60-plus game schedule was 13, by the 1950-51 Detroit Red Wings, who established the mark in 70 games.

But what made the Habs roster so impressive was that it was almost entirely homemade. With the exception of Mahovlich, every player on the roster was either drafted or developed by Montreal. Dryden and Doug Jarvis were drafted by other teams, but were dealt to the Canadiens before their NHL careers even began.

And to trace the lineage of that team, you have to go back a few years prior to the 1970-71 season, when the Canadiens shocked the hockey world by stunning the powerhouse Bruins in the first round of the playoffs en route to the Stanley Cup. They did it with Dryden, a rookie goaltender who had originally been drafted by the Bruins in 1964. At the 1970 draft, Pollock traded Ernie Hicke to the California Golden Seals for a swap of first round picks and helped seal California's fate as the last-place team by dealing Ralph Backstrom to the Los Angeles Kings at the deadline.

That allowed Pollock to draft Lafleur first overall, but then he took Murray Wilson 11th overall and Robinson in the No. 20 spot. With the 53rd overall selection, the Canadiens took Greg Hubick, who they flipped to get the rights to Jarvis four years later. All of those parts, along with what was already a formidable lineup in its own right, combined to make the team a juggernaut.

And although it might seem like the Habs didn't break a sweat that season, it wasn't as though they simply threw on the pads and played shinny for 60 minutes. In fact, the Bruins defeated Montreal in each of their first three meetings that season before the Canadiens took the final two. Even though they played 86.5 percent of the time that season either tied or in the lead, they trailed at one point in 21 of their 60 wins and in nine of their 12 ties. At one point in the campaign, they lost 7-2 to the St. Louis Blues and 7-3 to the Bruins in the space of five days.

But when the Canadiens won that season, they won big. They outscored their opponents by an average of almost 5-2 and 21 times that year they bested their opponent by five goals. Sixteen times the margin was six, nine times it was seven and four times they won by eight goals. And the scary thing about it was the Canadiens were so young. The only players on the roster who were over 30 were Jimmy Roberts and Yvan Cournoyer, who was beginning to be plagued by back troubles that caused him to miss 20 games and the entire playoffs, and forced him into retirement a year later. Lafleur and Shutt were just 24, Robinson was 25, Gainey and Doug Risebrough were 22 and Mario Tremblay was just 19.

That youthful enthusiasm, more than anything, kept Montreal from becoming complacent. It also helped that practices were intense and competitive, and that Bowman knew exactly what kind of mind games to play to keep the players constantly on edge.

"It's pretty simple," Mahovlich said. "Scotty never allowed us to get bored. Everybody talks about all the talent we had. But one of the things Scotty did very well was he knew how to manipulate that talent to make sure that talent was ready to play every night. We always had two or three extra players around who could take your spot in the lineup and the team wouldn't miss a beat.

"WE HAD A GREAT TEAM AND A GREAT RECORD, BUT THERE WERE AN INORDINATE NUMBER OF GAMES WHICH WE WON WITHOUT EVEN A REASONABLE AMOUNT OF DIFFICULTY. I'M HAPPY WE WON AS OFTEN AS WE DID. BUT I FOUND MYSELF SPENDING INCREASING TIME THINKING ABOUT WHAT I WANT TO DO WITH MY FUTURE."
– KEN DRYDEN

"Even though we were winning all the time, even if you had bumps and bruises, you kept playing because you were scared to death of losing your spot in the lineup. When you go through the first half of the season and you've lost only four or five games, it's the coach who creates the atmosphere where everybody is on pins and needles."

If there was one downside to that season, it was the squad was so dominant it spelled the beginning of the end of

Dryden's career. He was 29 years old at that time and had won so much by such a great margin, that it was during that season Dryden began to contemplate new challenges in his life.

"This isn't a complaint, but I didn't enjoy last season very much," Dryden said the next year. "We had a great team and a great record, but there were an inordinate number of games which we won without even a reasonable amount of difficulty. There were moments when we'd win a game and you'd go into the dressing room and there would be a certain amount of emptiness. Some guys would have to yell it up just to emphasize the fact we had won.

"I'm happy we won as often as we did and lost only eight times. But I found myself spending increasing time thinking about what I want to do with my future."

Perhaps it was a portent of things to come that the Canadiens' only two playoff losses came to the New York Islanders that spring. It would be another three seasons before the Islanders would usurp the Montreal dynasty with their first of four straight Stanley Cups. As dominant as those teams were, however, they were not the 1976-77 Canadiens, the standard by which all other great teams in the NHL will continue to be measured.

THE LEAGUE MIGHT AS WELL HAVE HELD ITS AWARDS CEREMONY AT THE CANADIENS TEAM BANQUET, SINCE LAFLEUR WON THE ART ROSS, HART AND CONN SMYTHE TROPHIES, DRYDEN AND MICHEL LAROCQUE THE VEZINA, ROBINSON THE NORRIS AND BOWMAN THE ADAMS.

Ken Dryden posted
four shutouts and a
1.55 GAA in 14 playoff
games in 1976–77.

No. 2
1983-84 EDMONTON OILERS

The Great One's 1984 Stanley Cup was the first of four consecutive years he would hoist the trophy at season's end.

WITH NAMES LIKE WAYNE GRETZKY, Mark Messier, Jari Kurri, Glenn Anderson, Grant Fuhr and Paul Coffey headlining the roster, you have to wonder how the 1983-84 Edmonton Oilers lost a game at all.

But at that time in history, the Oilers were still the new kids on the block. Four years into its NHL sojourn, Edmonton had won two Smythe Division titles and reached the Stanley Cup final once. The Oilers were built on offense and speed, setting goals-for records in '82 with 417 and again in '83 with 424, becoming the first NHL franchise to eclipse the 400-goal plateau.

"WE WERE JUST OBSESSED WITH ONE THING, THERE WAS ONE GOAL, ONE DESTINATION. WE LIVED IN THE MOMENT AS FAR AS THE SEASON WAS CONCERNED, BUT NOBODY DOUBTED FOR A MOMENT WHAT OUR OBJECTIVE WAS THAT YEAR."

– ANDY MOOG

Not only was the Oilers franchise young, but the players on the '83-84 roster were still in their early-to-mid-20s.

"Early on – '80, '81, '82, '83 – there was a little bit of naivety; we were all very young and inexperienced," explained goalie Andy Moog, who played 45 regular season and playoff games that season. "That burned off as we moved through to our first Cup final and lost to the Islanders the first time. Collectively we had our eyes opened about what commitment was and the Islanders demonstrated that to us in beating us the year before."

The young Oilers had been manhandled in the 1983 Cup final by the dynastic and more experienced New York Islanders. The question was already being asked: If 22-year-old phenom Gretzky – already a four-time Hart Trophy winner – never won a Stanley Cup, would his phenomenal individual career still rank up there with the all-time best?

In addition to the headliners, much of the supporting cast had outstanding years. Defensemen Charlie Huddy and Kevin Lowe both eclipsed the 40-point mark and provided Coffey with back-up. Up front, relative veteran Pat Hughes had the last – and best – productive season of his career with 27 goals and 55 points, while Dave Hunter scored more than 20 goals for the only time in his career. Ken Linseman, acquired from Hartford a year before, regressed in production, but proved his worth by finishing third on the team in the playoffs with 10 goals.

The young Oilers, now ravenous for a Stanley Cup, got off to a terrific start, winning their first seven games and 19 of their first 23. The first blip occurred in late-November and early December, when the Oilers lost four of seven. Hardly a skid, but it was something to improve on.

During their next 20 games, the Oilers lost only once, pulling well away from anyone in their division and showing nothing was going to slow a juggernaut that considered anything less than a championship a failure.

Edmonton did have its fair share of challenges, however. The team faced injury concerns when both Kurri and Messier went down. And even though the unheralded Hughes stepped up in response with five goals in a 10-5 win over the division rival Calgary Flames in early February, that didn't stop the Oilers from having to deal with their first losing streak of the season, a five-gamer, culminating in an 11-0 loss to Hartford, Edmonton's first shutout loss since March of 1981.

After that dreadful streak, the Oilers began piling up wins again, dropping only four of their final 22 games. Edmonton set franchise records for wins (59), points (119) and an NHL goals-for record for the third straight season at 446, averaging more than five per game; a record that still stands. The high-water marks meant little to Edmonton, however.

"'WE LOOKED AT THOSE GUYS AND THEY'RE ALL BATTERED AND BLEEDING AND THEY'RE DEAD TIRED.' THAT WAS THE ONE LESSON THEY LEARNED PRIOR TO WINNING THE STANLEY CUP."

– ROD PHILLIPS, FORMER PLAY-BY-PLAY MAN FOR THE OILERS

"We were just obsessed with one thing, there was one goal, one destination," Moog said. "We lived in the moment as far as the season was concerned, but nobody doubted for a moment what our objective was that year."

The Oilers began their Cup run by plowing through the Jets in three games, outscoring their opening-round opponent 18-7.

Wayne Gretzky scored a remarkable 87 goals and 205 points in 1983–84, but even more impressive is the fact that point total was only the fourth best of his career.

In the division final, Edmonton faced another strong team from the Smythe, the Calgary Flames. The year prior, Edmonton knocked out the Flames in five games in what was the first time the two Alberta teams had faced off in playoff action.

"Calgary – that was a defining moment for us," Moog said. "Very physical; it really initiated and began the Battle of Alberta."

After splitting at home, Edmonton headed south to Calgary. In taking both games, by scores of 3-2 and 5-3, Edmonton didn't blow away the competition as they were accustomed to, but by taking a 3-1 series advantage and heading home, it was hard to imagine Calgary getting back into it.

However, after back-to-back one-goal wins, the Flames forced Game 7 in Edmonton for the right to move on to the Campbell Conference final against the North Stars. Playing to their strengths and showcasing their maturity, Edmonton showed up in a big way, dumping the Flames 7-4.

With their provincial rivals behind them, Edmonton rolled over Minnesota in four games. The North Stars never stood a chance as Edmonton opened the series with a seven-goal game and outscored Minnesota 22-10 in the sweep.

And with that, the Oilers entered a Stanley Cup final rematch with the one team on which they wanted to exact revenge and steal the chalice from: the New York Islanders.

One year after being swept by the Isles, the Oilers were a different, more mature team.

"They really learned a lot from the Islanders when they lost in '82-'83," explained Rod Phillips, the original play-by-play man for the Oilers. "They realized when that series was over that they probably hadn't worked as hard as they needed to work. They had to learn how to play better defensively; they had to sacrifice more.

"The Islanders were very much responsible in making the Oilers a better team because they kind of showed them the way. I know, talking to a lot of players as time went on, they said they looked over at the Islanders after the last game when they got swept and the Oilers players said to themselves, 'We looked at those guys and they're all battered and bleeding and they're dead tired.' That was the one lesson they learned prior to winning the Stanley Cup."

The Oilers opened with a defensively sound effort in a 1-0 win in New York before dropping Game 2 by a 6-1 count. They headed home for the next three games with an outside chance to win their first Cup on home ice.

THE OILERS WERE BUILT ON OFFENSE AND SPEED, SETTING GOALS-FOR RECORDS IN '82 WITH 417 AND AGAIN IN '83 WITH 424, BECOMING THE FIRST NHL FRANCHISE TO ECLIPSE THE 400-GOAL PLATEAU.

With surprising back-to-back blowouts in Games 3 and 4 – both 7-2 counts – it was clear this Edmonton team was better-prepared mentally to face the veteran Isles, who had won four Cups in a row.

"My sense was we learned a lot about ourselves the year before and a little bit about strategy and tactics the year before," said Moog, now an assistant coach with the Dallas Stars. "I think it was (assistant coach) John Muckler who gave us a little insight in how to beat the Islanders up the ice and this was the early stages of trapping and backchecking and defensive-zone coverages. They had one subtle little change to our breakouts. Generally it was just the defense up the ice with speed and make a pass, but they made a subtle change to make an outlet pass early and played a give-and-go game and sort of broke the defensive scheme of the Islanders.

"We felt like we had an edge. We had all the experience, we had the youth and then we had an edge tactically: we knew how to beat them up the ice. There were a lot of rush goals scored by the Oilers in that series."

With one win to go before reaching their goal, Gretzky, the young Oilers captain, spoke to his teammates and explained just how much this last win would mean and inspired his team to push through the finish line.

"Wayne stood up in the dressing room before the (final) game and said all the individual awards he's won could never compare to winning the Stanley Cup," Messier said at the time. "That got everyone going and made us all realize how much it means to win the Stanley Cup."

In their last possible home game of the season, the Oilers were crowned as champions and slayers of the Islanders dynasty by winning the decisive game 5-2. Their offense-first mentality was a new way of attacking the game and many thought this was just the start of something big – perhaps a new dynasty was emerging and a new style along with it.

"I hope we influence the game further within the next five years," Gretzky said in '84. "First of all, we put people in buildings. I think people enjoy the way we play. We are a skating team. People come to watch us play and then go away from the rink feeling excited. I feel we can't do anything but help hockey and I'm very excited about that."

With eight goals and 26 points in 19 playoff games, Messier received his first and only Conn Smythe Trophy. Gretzky scored 87 goals and reached the 200-point plateau for the second time in his career (205), winning his fifth-straight Hart Trophy, fourth-straight Art Ross Trophy and third-straight Lester B. Pearson Award.

The 1983-84 Oilers have stood the test of time as one of hockey's best. Their championship started a run of five Cups in seven years and legitimately launched Gretzky into the debate surrounding the all-time best player.

But at the time, it was hard for the Oilers to comprehend and put into context just how good they were and where their place in history was.

"That run of two or three years in that program was exceptional," Moog explained. "Looking back now, we probably took ourselves a little bit for granted; it was just an exceptional group."

No. 3

1982-83 NEW YORK ISLANDERS

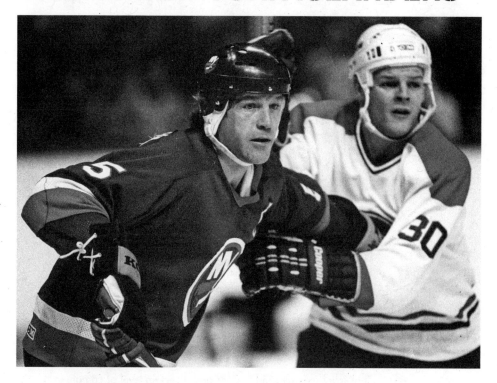

FROM THE OUTSIDE LOOKING IN, the casual observer might not think the 1982-83 New York Islanders were the best team the franchise has ever iced. But ask one of the best players in franchise history and he'll beg to differ.

"I think we were a machine at that point," said Hall of Fame defenseman Denis Potvin. "We were so grooved and so emotionally sharp. It was just such a joy to play; everything was automatic."

When the '82-83 season began, the Islanders were the favorite to win their fourth consecutive Stanley Cup and match the 1970s Montreal Canadiens, who won from '76 through '79. Twenty out of 20 NHL experts polled by THN before the 1982 season picked the Islanders to win the Patrick Division; THN also named them the Cup favorites.

When the Islanders' Denis Potvin retired, he was the all-time leader in goals and points for defensemen.

"THE OILERS ARE SO DAMN COCKY. EDMONTON DOESN'T RESPECT ANYONE. THERE ISN'T ANY ONE TEAM WE WANT TO BEAT MORE."

– BOB BOURNE

The Islanders were stacked, led by one of the greatest two-way players in league history, the calming Bryan Trottier; the super-confident Mike Bossy, who seemed able to score at will; team captain and three-time Norris Trophy winner Potvin, a man who oozed confidence; all-time grinder Clark Gillies; and goaltender Billy Smith, seemingly able to will himself to victory. Behind the bench, the Islanders were led by coach Al Arbour; pulling the strings was GM Bill Torrey. All seven of those men are Hall of Famers.

The supporting cast included the likes of John Tonelli, a gritty playmaker with a scorer's touch, and 1981 Conn Smythe winner Butch Goring, along with top-six worthy forwards Brent and Duane Sutter, and the Bobs – Nystrom and Bourne.

But the campaign didn't exactly go swimmingly. Potvin held out during the pre-season, looking for a better contract. A compromise was reached and the Islanders shot out of the gate, winning 11 of their first 13 contests. But the schedule didn't make it easy on the team. The Isles played 34 games in 67 days to begin the season, a compact schedule that would have today's players up in arms.

That schedule, nagging injuries and a certain level of complacency conspired to send the team into a funk that lasted much of the season. The Islanders won just four of 16 November games and four of 12 in December; that after winning Presidents' Trophies and registering a plus-230 in goals the previous two seasons.

As the calendar turned from 1982 to '83, many were saying the Islanders had reached their apex and were no longer the team to beat. The first game of the New Year was a loss to Pittsburgh that dropped the Islanders to second place in the division for the first time in three years. And it was their 16th loss of the campaign, matching the team's total from the season prior.

Arbour, the master tactician who always kept his guys humble, hadn't settled on anything resembling set lines and the goaltending duo of Smith – the reigning Vezina Trophy winner – and Rollie Melanson split games, with the latter actually finishing with better numbers by season's end. New York dipped as low as third in its division. To say there was dissension in the room may be a bit strong, but frustration among the players was at an all-time high. One thing that was gone was the complacency.

"I certainly felt I didn't play like a first-team all-star during the first half of the season," said Bossy, who had endured the longest goal drought of his career to that point, but still finished with 118 points and became the first player in NHL history to score 60-plus goals three straight seasons.

In March things changed. And during the final six weeks of the season, the Islanders turned a corner and began playing a game reminiscent of Cup seasons past. Lines were set, injuries healed and the stars – although they'd been putting up what today would be outstanding numbers – began playing like stars again. The Islanders were back – and hungry.

"You would watch us play...and see the puck pursuit," Potvin said of the team defense. "All of those things you talk about to-day: the gap between defense and forward, the work down low in our own zone. We were stifling.

"And on offense we were devastating. We could really create some offense. We were really good on the power play. I never had to look up and say 'Where am I moving the puck? All those things were boom-boom automatic.

"Everybody was grooved."

That they were. The Islanders rolled into the post-season on a high.

In the first round they faced the Washington Capitals, who they had battled for second in the division all season and finished just two points ahead of; 10 points behind the Philadelphia Flyers. The Caps boasted seven 20-goal scorers, but managed just a single win in the best-of-five series.

Then came the New York Rangers, who had dispatched the division champs and second-overall Flyers in a three-game sweep, in the Patrick Division final. This was the heyday of the Empire State rivalry. The two teams had played each other in the post-season three of the previous four years.

The Rangers were the glory team, playing under the bright lights of Manhattan with all the history that came with being an Original Six team, but were Cup-less since 1940. The bedroom-community Islanders were the dynasty team, winning three consecutive Cups on the heels of those great Montreal Canadiens teams. Rangers fans were aghast; Islanders fans couldn't help but rub it in.

Against the Blueshirts, the stars played well, but weren't the difference. The Islanders' depth took the series over. Bourne and the Sutters led the way. Bourne's 12 points against the Rangers was a franchise record; his end-to-end Game 5 winner was the seminal moment of the six-game Islanders win.

"I've never done anything like that before," Bourne said of his goal after the season. "When I got home I watched it 10 or 12 times...I'll save that tape the rest of my life."

With the Rangers once again out-classed and relegated to an afterthought, the Islanders moved on to face the 50-victory, President's Trophy-winning Boston Bruins in the Wales Conference final. This time the team's stars shone. And Bossy shone brighter than any other.

> ## "I THINK WE WERE A MACHINE AT THAT POINT. WE WERE SO GROOVED AND SO EMOTIONALLY SHARP. IT WAS JUST SUCH A JOY TO PLAY; EVERYTHING WAS AUTOMATIC."
> – DENIS POTVIN

The right winger tied a then NHL playoff record with nine goals in the series, punctuating it all with four markers in the deciding sixth game, an 8-4 trouncing. The series victory set up a marquee Cup final against the superstar-laden Edmonton Oilers.

Edmonton had set an NHL record, scoring 424 goals during the regular season, 122 more than the Isles and an average of 5.3 scores per contest. With 71 goals and 196 points, Wayne Gretzky had won the scoring title by a jaw-dropping 72 points. Edmonton's murderers' row also included Mark Messier, Jari Kurri and Glenn Anderson, all of whom tallied 45-plus goals and 100-plus points. Defenseman Paul Coffey rounded out Edmonton's top-five with 29 goals and 96 points of his own; four other Oilers also managed 19 or more goals.

Duane Sutter, one of six brothers to play in the NHL, was the Islanders' 1979 first round pick (17th overall) and won the Stanley Cup in each of his first four seasons.

The Islanders entered the Cup final with a point to prove. The young Oilers were a brash group, itching to win their first Cup and offering no quarter or nod to history along the way.

"We want to beat (the Oilers) more than anything," Gillies said before the series. "They think they're the greatest thing since the invention of sliced bread."

Added Bourne: "The Oilers are so damn cocky. Edmonton doesn't respect anyone. There isn't any one team we want to beat more."

And beat the Oilers they did. In historic fashion.

New York swept the series in four games, scoring 17 goals along the way and holding the vaunted Edmonton attack to just six with a dogged determination to play tough team defense. The Great One himself managed just four points, all of them assists. Fittingly, the top individual accolade went to the goalie as Battlin' Billy was named the Conn Smythe Trophy winner, the fourth different recipient in four years for the Isles.

The 1983 Cup made the Islanders one of the most dominant teams ever. They made it back to their fifth final in a row in 1984, winning a record 19 consecutive post-season series en route, which only added to the argument. There they again met Edmonton, but the Oilers were simply too much; or, rather, the Islanders had had too much. Edmonton prevailed in five games to end to New York's attempt at matching the 1950s Canadiens with five Cups in succession.

"There's no question," Potvin said when asked if the Islanders were simply worn out by the time the 1984 final rolled around. "Consider this: Montreal won five Cups by winning 10 playoff series. You couldn't ask the NHL to make it more difficult."

With an eye to penny-pinching, the league also put a 2-3-2 game schedule into effect in 1984, a measure meant to save the teams money on travel.

"That was ridiculous," Potvin said. "We had to spend eight days in Edmonton. (The fans) circled our hotel with pick-up trucks… day in and day out."

The Islanders lost all three of those games.

"For us it was huge, because we were hurting, we were tired," Potvin noted. "And then five consecutive finals. And we also played the 1981 Canada Cup, we were involved in all the All-Star Games."

It's not sour grapes on Potvin's part. He was quick to say he didn't necessarily think his Islanders were better, even than the 1983 Oilers team, but you could hear the frustration in his voice three decades later. He truly felt that Islanders team could have won a fifth title if circumstances had been a little different.

"I think we played 120 playoff games in five years," Potvin said. "How many NHLers in history have played 120 playoff games? And we did it in five consecutive years."

No. 4

1955-56 MONTREAL CANADIENS

AS DIFFICULT AS IT MAY BE TO BELIEVE, there was a time in NHL history when the Toronto Maple Leafs were neck-and-neck with the Montreal Canadiens when it came to Stanley Cup championships.

Coach Toe Blake got to sip from the Cup after his first year behind the Montreal Canadiens bench.

Seriously.

It was during the Korean War, but it happened. In fact, when the Canadiens won the seventh Stanley Cup in franchise history in 1953, they actually pulled to within one of the Maple Leafs as the NHL's championship standard bearers.

That all changed in 1956. Not only did the Canadiens catch the Leafs, they touched off a flurry of five straight Cups that pulled them away from the rest of the pack for good. That they did so in such dominating fashion and with such a mind-boggling array of talent makes them one of the greatest teams of all-time.

What made them so dominant? Well, four players on the first all-star team might be an indication. Or the fact the NHL changed its rules in response to the Canadiens juggernaut of a power play would give you a pretty good idea.

Of the four Canadiens' Stanley Cup winners that followed, none won as many games, gave up fewer goals or totaled as many points as the 1955-56 team that touched off the most dominating dynasty the NHL has ever seen. There were a number of reasons for that, but the most prominent among them was Jean Beliveau's emergence as a big, mean, dominating player who succeeded in sending a message to the rest of the NHL and making all kinds of room for himself.

OF THE FOUR CANADIENS' STANLEY CUP WINNERS THAT FOLLOWED, NONE WON AS MANY GAMES, GAVE UP FEWER GOALS OR TOTALED AS MANY POINTS AS THE 1955-56 TEAM THAT TOUCHED OFF THE MOST DOMINATING DYNASTY THE NHL HAS EVER SEEN.

Playing on a line with Bert Olmstead on the left and Bernie Geoffrion at right wing, Beliveau scored a career-high 47 goals that season and piled up a phenomenal 143 penalty minutes. It marked only the second time in league history – after Nels Stewart exactly 30 years before – that a player led the league in goals and points and had 100 PIM.

Gordie Howe and Mario Lemieux matched the feat after Beliveau, but in the history of the NHL, only Stan Mikita, with 146 PIM in 1963-64 and 154 in 1964-65, has piled up more penalty minutes in a season in which he won the Art Ross Trophy.

"Whoever you are, coming out of the minors, the step is pretty high to the NHL," Beliveau said. "You look at some of the great players and it took them a few years to adjust to the speed. For me, it was the same thing. And I guess you could say I got a little bit more assertive. I decided at that time that I had the size and I had to use it a little bit more. It was then that I decided to play this game a little more physically."

Beliveau also heard and read that he was passing the puck too much and took the words to heart. Being a playmaker until that time, Beliveau decided to shoot more and it resulted in scoring totals he never again matched. Much of the success could be attributed to Olmstead, who led the league with 56 assists that season (most of which came on Beliveau goals). Known as one of the more ornery and hard-working players of his time, if Olmstead ever saw Beliveau in the corner, he'd growl, "Get the hell out of here and get in front of the net."

Much the way the best leaders in the game do today, Olmstead constantly pushed Beliveau and Geoffrion to be better and more determined players. Beliveau said he and Geoffrion would often come off the ice thinking they had had a productive shift, only to hear the exact opposite from the 29-year-old veteran.

"He made us mad because whatever we did after our shift, (he thought) we could have done better," Beliveau said. "And it was after my career I realized I probably played the best hockey of my career with Geoffrion and Olmstead. He made us mad, but he made us better players."

Olmstead, who was enshrined in the Hockey Hall of Fame 13 years after Beliveau and Geoffrion were in 1972, said his two linemates were quick studies and willing learners.

"I GUESS YOU COULD SAY I GOT A LITTLE BIT MORE ASSERTIVE. I DECIDED AT THAT TIME THAT I HAD THE SIZE AND I HAD TO USE IT A LITTLE BIT MORE. IT WAS THEN THAT I DECIDED TO PLAY THIS GAME A LITTLE MORE PHYSICALLY."

– JEAN BELIVEAU

"You could see right from the beginning that the skill was there with both of them," Olmstead said. "But the thing that impressed me so much was that they were willing to work so hard. They never lipped off and they learned and learned and that's why they turned out to be such super players."

It also helped that the Canadiens had a second line made up of rookie Henri Richard at center with his all-world brother Maurice on the right wing and Hall of Famer Dickie Moore on the left.

And check out this power play – Olmstead, Beliveau and Rocket Richard up front with Doug Harvey and Geoffrion at the points. It was a power play so dominating that, as a result of Beliveau scoring three power play goals in 44 seconds in a Nov. 5 game against the Boston Bruins, the league changed its rules to mandate that once a power play goal was scored, the penalized player comes out of the penalty box.

"I got all three of those goals against (Terry) Sawchuk," Beliveau said. "A pretty good goalie."

There were a lot of factors that led to the 1955-56 Stanley Cup, not the least of which was the fact that prior to that season, the Canadiens had been in the previous five Stanley Cup finals, but had just one Cup to show for it. That included two straight seven-game defeats at the hands of the Detroit Red Wings, including 1954 when a Tony Leswick dump-in in overtime of Game 7 glanced off Harvey's glove and past a beleaguered Gerry McNeil.

> ## "WE HAD JEAN, WHO COULD FIRE THE PUCK LIKE A HOWITZER AND HENRI WOULD CHASE EVERYONE ALL OVER THE ICE. THEY WERE TOTALLY DIFFERENT, BUT THEY WERE GREAT. YOU'D NEVER HEAR A WORD FROM HENRI ON THE BENCH AND IT WAS THE SAME IN THE DRESSING ROOM. HE WAS LIKE A LITTLE MOUSE...UNTIL HE STEPPED ON THE ICE."
>
> – BERT OLMSETAD ON JEAN BELIVEAU AND HENRI RICHARD

The Canadiens had played the Red Wings incredibly evenly the previous two seasons, going 6-6-2 against Detroit in 1953-54 while scoring 27 goals and giving up 27. In '54-55, they went 7-7-0 against the Wings while scoring and giving up 38 goals. The Canadiens finished just two points behind the Red Wings in the standings and one win away from the Stanley Cup, largely because of the infamous, playoff-long suspension to Rocket Richard for punching a linesman during an altercation.

But the next season, Montreal piled up an 8-4-2 record against Detroit and outscored them by nine en route to a 100-point season and a 24-point lead on the Wings, who had finished on top of the regular season standings each of the previous seven seasons.

The relative lack of success cost Dick Irvin his job as coach and after he left for Chicago, the Canadiens hired former great Toe Blake to coach the team. Blake was a stickler for detail – he insisted on each player weighing in every day – and was something of a taskmaster, but the players respected Blake and were willing to do whatever it took to make him successful.

"The players really liked Toe," Beliveau said. "As long as the players were working and giving an effort, Toe had no problems with you and he knew the puck would go in sooner or later."

He was certainly right about that. Beliveau, Maurice Richard and Olmstead finished 1-3-4 in scoring and Geoffrion was seventh. Harvey led all defensemen in points en route to his second of seven Norris Trophies.

It turns out, though, that Beliveau was simply warming up for the playoffs. In 10 post-season games, he scored 12 goals, including seven in the Stanley Cup final.

Maurice 'Rocket' Richard was second on the Montreal Canadiens and third in the league with 71 points in 70 games in 1955–56.

There is little doubt the Canadiens were blessed with a plethora of strength, particularly at center. With Beliveau anchoring the first line and Henri Richard the second, the Canadiens had a punch down the middle that could not be equaled. Beliveau and Richard would go on to play together on the Canadiens for another 15 seasons, with Beliveau winning a total of 10 Cups and Richard, a league-record 11.

"We had Jean, who could fire the puck like a Howitzer and Henri would chase everyone all over the ice," Olmstead said. "They were totally different, but they were great. You'd never hear a word from Henri on the bench and it was the same in the dressing room. He was like a little mouse...until he stepped on the ice."

If the Canadiens needed anything else going for them, they had a united cause beyond dethroning the Red Wings as the league's best team. Veteran defenseman Butch Bouchard, one of the lynchpins of the teams in the 1940s that saved the franchise from oblivion, was playing his last season and was team captain.

Think, to a lesser extent, Ray Bourque with the Colorado Avalanche. Bouchard played just 36 games during the regular season and one in the playoffs – the game in which the Canadiens clinched the Cup. Bouchard received only a couple of shifts in the game, but was out there for the last one and skated off the ice for the last time with the Stanley Cup in his arms.

There's little doubt, however, the metamorphosis of Beliveau into a superstar player in the league was the driving force that powered the Canadiens in 1955-56.

"It was a case of a promising player," Olmstead said, "finally coming to the front."

No. 5

1951-52 DETROIT RED WINGS

Terry Sawchuk was unbeatable at home for the Detroit Red Wings and didn't allow a goal on Olympia ice during the playoffs.

OF ALL THAT WAS ACHIEVED BY THE 1951-52 EDITION of the Detroit Red Wings, no accomplishment had more staying power than their ability to turn a slimy sea creature from a dining delicacy into a symbol of dominance.

It was during the second period of the Cup-clinching fourth game that an octopus was first fired onto the ice at Olympia, the Wings' home rink.

Beyond some sharp-witted theories from media members pertaining to the reason for the bizarre visitor's appearance, the octopus also prompted what is surely one of the most unique public address requests in the history of sport: "Octopi shall not occupy the ice. Please refrain from throwing same."

Legendary sportswriter Elmer Ferguson suggested it was a shame the octopus couldn't play center, because the visiting Montreal Canadiens were desperately in need of one.

"FOR THE FIRST FIVE YEARS OF HIS CAREER HE WAS THE GREATEST GOALTENDER WHO EVER PLAYED, BUT HE WAS A SQUIRRELY INDIVIDUAL."

– TED LINDSAY ON TERRY SAWCHUK

But once the correlation between eight arms and the eight games it took for Detroit to sweep its way to a championship was made, tentacles became part of a Hockeytown tradition that exists to this day.

Not only did the Wings go 8-0 in dropping the Toronto Maple Leafs and the Habs en route to claiming the Cup, 22-year-old sophomore goalie Terry Sawchuk also didn't allow a goal in four games at Olympia. Overall, he stopped 213 of 218 shots faced in the playoffs and went 277 minutes and 54 seconds of post-season play without allowing a goal at home.

That stingy goaltending provided the backbone for a Detroit club that won four Cups in a six-year period between 1949-50 and 1954-55 and finished first overall in seven straight seasons.

Coach Tommy Ivan said a big reason for Sawchuk's success was slimming down his robust frame. He was 226 pounds when he showed up to training camp for what would be a rookie-of-the-year campaign in 1950, eventually working down to 193. The goalie was 219 pounds to kick off camp in 1951 and used a diet that consisted mostly of double orders of medium steaks coupled with milk and lettuce to reduce that figure to 183 pounds by the last game of the season.

"Terry swears he starved at the dinner table in order to feast on shutouts," wrote Marshall Dann in The Hockey News.

Born of Ukrainian descent, Sawchuk was as good as they came in the crease, but was also susceptible to notorious and severe mood swings.

"For the first five years of his career he was the greatest goaltender who ever played, but he was a squirrely individual," said legendary Wings left winger Ted Lindsay, now 85.

One Wing who got a very firsthand glimpse at Sawchuk's volatile behavioral patterns was Marty Pavelich, whose seat in the dressing room was right beside the puckstopper's. Pavelich soon learned it was best to take a wait-and-see approach when dealing with Sawchuk.

"Marty used to sit next to him and call him 'the Uke,' " Lindsay said. "(Sawchuk) would come in for a week or 10 days and say, 'Hi Marty,' then for a week he wouldn't say anything.

"So Marty decided, 'I'll wait till he talks to me; I won't talk to him.' "

Nevertheless, his incredible reflexes made stopping pucks like picking cherries for Sawchuk.

"You could throw a handful of rice at him and he'd catch every grain," Lindsay said.

Not that Sawchuk was the only special player on the team. Superstar Gordie Howe led the league with 47 goals and 86 points in 70 games, with Lindsay's 69 points ranking him second.

The two men flanked veteran center Sid Abel to form 'The Production Line,' the most feared trio in hockey at the time. The Wings' top unit paced the entire NHL with a combined 94 goals between them. Lindsay, who led the '52 playoffs with five goals, said the key to the line's success was Abel's understanding that his two wingers each required different buttons to be pushed.

"I had to be curtailed as far as my enthusiasm and Gordie, you'd think he might be asleep over there," Lindsay said. "That's how relaxed he was, until he got the puck."

Lindsay was 27 years old when the Wings lifted the '52 Cup, while Howe had just turned 24. The 34-year-old Abel's role in their lives went beyond passing them the puck; he provided stability and support off the ice, too.

THE WINGS WERE DOMINANT AT BOTH ENDS OF THE ICE, SCORING MORE GOALS (215) AND ALLOWING FEWER (133) THAN ANY OTHER CLUB.

"Sid was our father image because we were both young," Lindsay said. "Sid had talent, but he was a little older.

"He had a wonderful wife named Gloria, an Italian woman who knew how to cook pasta. We used to go there a lot for dinner."

Coached by Ivan, the Red Wings established a new league mark with 101 points during the 1950-51 season, but were beaten by Montreal in the playoffs' opening round. That provided extra incentive for the 1951-52 outfit, which finished with exactly 100 points. A pair of key additions helped ensure Detroit wouldn't suffer the same fate as the previous season's club.

First, GM Jack Adams traded Gaye Stewart to the New York Rangers for Tony Leswick, who had nine goals in the regular season, but three in just eight playoff games. The offense was a bonus, but, as Adams noted, he acquired Leswick for his defensive prowess.

"During the season, he scored three goals that won games for us," Adams said at the time. "And there's no telling how much wear and tear he's saved on Red Kelly. Red hasn't had to kill off the penalties, as he did before we got Leswick. It's been a good deal for us."

The other prominent new addition was Alex Delvecchio, who scored a respectable 15 goals and 37 points in 65 games as one of five rookies on the team.

The Wings were dominant at both ends of the ice, scoring more goals (215) and allowing fewer (133) than any other club. Detroit went undefeated in its first 15 games on the road.

In addition to the Art Ross Trophy, Howe also took home the Hart Trophy as league MVP, while Sawchuk claimed the Vezina. Howe, Sawchuk, Lindsay and Kelly were all named first-team all-stars.

After posting a winning record against each team both at home and as the visitor in the regular season, the Wings upped the

ante in the playoffs, becoming the first team to win the Cup in just eight games since the six-team league went to two best-of-seven series in 1943. The only other club to win a title in the minimum eight contests before 1967 expansion is the 1960 Canadiens.

In all, the Wings trailed for a total of 99 seconds in the 1952 playoffs.

"That's the best Detroit team I've ever handled – best by far," Adams said in the Wings dressing room after the Cup-clinching game. "When you put legs and heart together you've really got something."

Detroit remained a league power through the mid-50s, until some highly questionable decisions by Adams triggered a decline. After winning the Cup in '55, Adams stunned the hockey world by trading Sawchuk to Boston in a deal that involved nine players in total. Though he was re-acquired two years later, Detroit didn't win another Cup for more than 40 years.

Despite the best efforts of Henri Richard and the Montreal Canadiens, Marty Pavelich and his Detroit Red Wings teammates steamrolled through the Cup final 4–0.

Adams also famously dealt Lindsay to Chicago in 1957 after 'Terrible Ted' angered him by trying to gather support among his fellow players to form a union.

Another huge blunder on Adams' part, according to Lindsay, was trading Kelly, a standout blueliner, to the New York Rangers in 1960. Kelly, 32 at the time, refused to go along with the trade, opting to retire instead and return home to his tobacco farm. Lindsay said his old teammate's decision was outside the bounds of what any hockey power broker at the time thought possible.

"That was an insult to management because no player had enough money or was intelligent enough to know what to do with himself if he retired," he said. "That's what they thought of us."

With Kelly sticking to his guns, King Clancy, who worked under Leafs GM Conn Smythe, pitched a different notion to Adams.

"Clancy went to Adams and said, 'If I can talk him out of retirement, let's make a deal and you can get something for him,' " Lindsay said.

Five days after he was supposed to be a Ranger, Kelly became a Maple Leaf, moved up to center from his natural position of defense and won four more Cups in Toronto to match the four he won in Detroit.

As for the glory days in the Motor City, Lindsay says if that crew got back together they might add a couple more Cups to the mantle.

"We could still be playing today and never lose a game," he said. "That's how good we were."

"THAT WAS AN INSULT TO MANAGEMENT BECAUSE NO PLAYER HAD ENOUGH MONEY OR WAS INTELLIGENT ENOUGH TO KNOW WHAT TO DO WITH HIMSELF IF HE RETIRED. THAT'S WHAT THEY THOUGHT OF US."

– TED LINDSAY TALKING ABOUT RED KELLY RETIRING BEFORE ACCEPTING A TRADE TO THE NEW YORK RANGERS

No. 6

1971-72 BOSTON BRUINS

Phil Esposito's 66 goals and 133 points led both the Bruins and the league by wide margins in 1971–72.

THEY OWNED ONE OF THE GREAT SPORTS CITIES in North America.

The Boston Celtics were in the process of winning 11 NBA titles between 1957 and 1969, with a couple more to come in the mid-1970s. The 'Impossible Dream' Red Sox revived what had become a sleepy, somber baseball market. The Patriots still had their issues, but at least they'd been merged into the NFL and were moving out of a series of temporary Boston homes into a stadium in the suburbs.

But none of those franchises could touch the Boston Bruins of the late 1960s and early '70s that culminated with their second Stanley Cup championship in three years in 1971-72.

Phil Esposito, Johnny 'Chief' Bucyk, Derek 'Turk' Sanderson, John 'Pie' McKenzie, Gerry 'Cheesie' Cheevers and, of course, Bobby Orr didn't just rule the region, they inspired a group of New Englanders who helped engineer an Olympic Miracle (Jim Craig, Mike Eruzione, Dave Silk and Jack O'Callahan) and spawned a generation of Boston-area players who put the U.S. on the international hockey map (Jeremy Roenick, Keith Tkachuk, Brian Leetch, Tom Barrasso, Tony Amonte, etc.).

The starting point was the incomparable Orr, whose name was well known long before he got to Boston. Die-hard fans – and the franchise itself – hung their hopes on the wunderkind whose rights were obtained at age 14 when the Bruins locked him up by sponsoring his minor hockey team. Out of the playoffs since 1959, Boston at least had something to look forward to.

The savior finally arrived in 1966-67 at the age of 18. While he was nearly everything he was supposed to be, Orr still wasn't enough. The Bruins, coached for the first time by nearly as fresh a face as Orr's – Harry Sinden, age 34 – finished last in the NHL despite Orr's Calder Trophy, second all-star season.

Fortunately, a critical link to Boston's long-ago Golden Era was still in place.

THE STARTING POINT WAS THE INCOMPARABLE ORR, WHOSE NAME WAS WELL KNOWN LONG BEFORE HE GOT TO BOSTON.

Hall of Famer Milt Schmidt, who centered the famous 'Kraut Line' that led Boston to Cups in 1939 and 1941, had just finished his second stint coaching the talent-challenged Bruins in 1965-66 when team president Weston Adams Sr. made him GM. Schmidt knew some talent was in place (especially in goal, where Cheevers and Ed Johnston were far better than their statistics suggested), but he also knew he had to surround Orr with more.

Schmidt found a trade partner in Chicago's Tommy Ivan, whose Blackhawks finished first in the NHL during the regular season, but were upset by the New York Rangers in the first playoff round. On May 15, 1967, Schmidt obtained 24-year-old Phil

The Bruins 'Terrible' Ted Green was as tough as they come and helped the B's to their second of two Cups in three years.

Esposito, who had just scored nearly a point per game (21 goals, 61 points in 69 games), and a pair of little-used, 22-year-old forwards in Ken Hodge and Fred Stanfield for forward Pit Martin, defenseman Gilles Marotte and goalie Jack Norris.

The team that became known as the Big, Bad Bruins was nearly complete, save for one more essential ingredient – colorful center Derek Sanderson, who won the Calder the year after Orr.

With more talent on the roster, a playing field somewhat leveled by the NHL and Sinden proving to be an impeccable match-maker, the '67-68 Bruins earned the first of an unprecedented 29 consecutive playoff berths. Ex-Chicago teammates Esposito and Hodge played on the top line. Sinden plugged Stanfield between the long-suffering Bucyk and the fiery McKenzie – they finished 2-3-4 in team scoring behind Esposito, who was No. 2 in the NHL with 35 goals and 84 points. The brash young Sanderson played on a checking line that included stately, steady Ed Westfall.

Besides Orr, the defense was largely anonymous, but was also tough (Ted Green, Don Awrey and Gary Doak all hit 100 penalty minutes) and capable, too. Orr, already experiencing the knee problems that would doom him to a too-brief career, only played 46 games, but was still so far ahead of the pack he won the first of eight straight Norris Trophies.

"I THINK WE SHOULD HAVE WON THREE STANLEY CUPS IN A ROW. IT'S STILL VERY DISAPPOINTING...BUT YOU LOOK BACK, AND THERE WERE SO MANY GOOD TIMES IN THOSE DAYS, SO MANY GREAT TEAMS."

– FRED STANFIELD

The '68-69 Bruins were an offensive powerhouse; the first NHL team to top 300 goals, with Esposito becoming the first player in league history to reach the 100-point mark – and then some. There was still nearly a month left in the season when the big, impossible-to-move center hit triple digits; he'd tally 26 more to close the season with 126 points, a then-record 77 assists and win the Hart Trophy as NHL MVP.

By now, Sinden had crafted one of history's most-feared power plays, with Bucyk, Esposito and Hodge up front, Orr at the right point and Stanfield on the left. The Bruins were also a threat to score when shorthanded with talents like Orr and Sanderson, the latter easily at least a No. 2 center on nearly any other team in the league.

"However you wanted to play," Orr said recently, "we could do it. Physical, skilled...I mean, our team was just so good."

Offensive exploits notwithstanding, the Bruins were still building toward a championship. One playoff round in '68 became two in '69 (Montreal, en route to Cups both years, eliminated the B's) and by 1970, Boston wasn't to be denied. Orr, healthy enough to begin a run of three uninterrupted seasons, became the first defenseman to lead the team in scoring with 120 points (and a team high 125 penalty minutes). Players like Wayne Cashman (ultimately a fixture on the Esposito-Hodge line), Garnet 'Ace' Bailey and Wayne Carleton grew into key support roles. The defense corps managed to survive the season-long loss of Green, whose skull was fractured in a pre-season, stick-swinging incident with Wayne Maki.

Only the New York Rangers, who edged Montreal for the fourth and final East Division playoff slot (they finished only seven points behind Boston, which lost a tiebreaker with Chicago for first place), put up a post-season fight. The Blueshirts took the Bruins to six games in a fight-filled first round, but once Boston broke a 2-2 tie in the series, it was over. The only compelling storyline in a four-game semifinal sweep over Chicago was Esposito's match-up against his brother, Black Hawks goalie Tony. And there was little drama in the Cup final until the very, very end of that four-game sweep. Orr, after pinching down the boards to stop a St. Louis breakout, worked a give-and-go with Sanderson and scored perhaps the best-remembered goal in Cup history (it certainly produced the best photograph) at 40 seconds of overtime. After 29 years, the Stanley Cup had returned to Boston.

Two years later, it was back again, after the highly motivated Bruins gutted out a tough, six-game final against the Rangers.

There's no mystery as to why the Bruins didn't follow that '72 Cup with more: Orr's knees continued to deteriorate and, in large part because of his trust in agent Alan Eagleson, his relationship with the Bruins deteriorated, too. His knees all but destroyed (Orr played only 10 games in 1975-76), he signed with Chicago as a free agent in '76-77. Orr's condition wasn't the only factor. The World Hockey Association lured some of Boston's most popular players away after the '72 championship – Sanderson,

Cheevers (18-3 during the two Cup runs; forever remembered for the stitch-mark themed facemask), McKenzie and Green. Further NHL expansion ate into Boston's roster as well.

But if anything gnaws at the Bruins of that era, it's that they didn't win in 1971. Just two years after becoming the first NHL team to score 300 goals, they missed the 400-goal mark by a single tally. Esposito (152 points), Orr (139; 102 on assists), Bucyk (116) and Hodge (105) finished 1-2-3-4 in league scoring and 10 Bruins hit the 20-goal mark ("That was when 20 goals was pretty big, too," Orr said.). The Bruins, 26-0-1 at cramped, beloved Boston Garden at one point, became the first NHL team to win 50 games.

Sinden hadn't coached them, though: Denied what he felt was a fair raise after 1970, he left hockey for two years, until returning to succeed Schmidt as GM in 1972. And no matter how powerful they may have been in those days, it rarely mattered when the playoff opponent was Montreal: The Bruins had lost 10 straight post-season series to the Canadiens by the time the 1971 first round matchup was set – and that just happened to be Ken Dryden's coming-out party. Boston finally seemed to have solved the gangly rookie Esposito called "a giraffe" with a 7-3 victory that gave them a 3-2 lead in the series, but the Habs won the next two and were off to win their third Cup in four years.

"We basically blew it," said Dallas Smith, Orr's frequent defense partner. "The next year we knew we had to use our heads a little more."

Added Stanfield: "I think we should have won three Stanley Cups in a row. It's still very disappointing...But you look back, and there were so many good times in those days, so many great teams. You feel bad not winning that third Cup – but we came back strong the next year, didn't we?"

"HOWEVER YOU WANTED TO PLAY, WE COULD DO IT. PHYSICAL, SKILLED...I MEAN, OUR TEAM WAS JUST SO GOOD."

– BOBBY ORR

No. 7

1974-75 PHILADELPHIA FLYERS

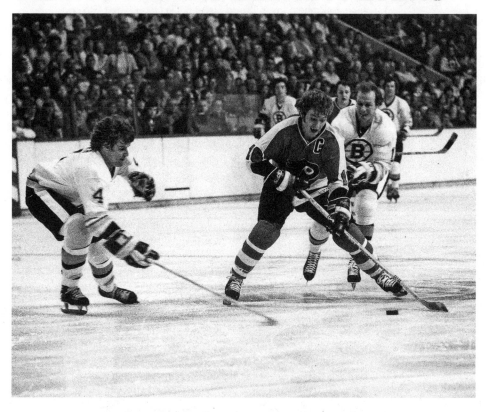

WHEN FRED SHERO WROTE THE FAMOUS "Win today and we walk together forever" line on his office message board the morning of May 19, 1974, little did the coach know his Flyers team would not only win a Stanley Cup that day, but, on the way down that eternal stroll, another the following year.

Togetherness. Ask any Flyer who played on the 1974-75 championship team what the key was to their success and that's the answer you get.

They didn't just play hockey as a group. They went to lunch after practice, socialized on days off, tipped a few after a hard-fought win and vacationed at the same spots on the Jersey shore in the summer.

Bobby Clarke won two Stanley Cups and three Hart Trophies during his career with the Flyers.

Corny as it might sound, it was a family. It was the last all-Canadian team to win a Stanley Cup, not that Americans or Europeans had started knocking down doors yet around the NHL, but there was a still sense of comrades-in-arms.

These Flyers had all the tactical elements – skill, speed, experience, toughness (as in Broad Street Bullies toughness) – to capture a title.

Yet without that camaraderie, that *esprit de corps*, the rare feat of back-to-back crowns (only five other teams have achieved it since) might not have happened.

Going into that second season, Shero knew repeating the Cinderella 1973-74 season would not be easy. Too many things could go wrong, as the 1975-76 Flyers – perhaps what would have been the strongest team in franchise history – would find out when Hall of Fame goaltender Bernie Parent went down with an injury.

So Shero, always a proponent of challenging a hockey player's intellect rather than his physical talents, worked harder than ever at the mind game. He watched film of the Soviet Red Army team (a squad his 1976 Flyers would beat to salvage NHL pride), how it played as a cohesive unit and instituted those same principles.

At the same time, he encouraged his players to interact practically all of their waking hours.

GM Keith Allen is credited with being the architect of this first expansion team to win a Cup, and then two, but Shero, nicknamed "Freddie the Fog" for his tinted glasses, unconventional methods and innovative ways – such as hiring Mike Nykoluk as the NHL's first prominent assistant coach – was the mastermind.

"WE HAD A LOT OF TALENT – LOTS OF TEAMS HAVE TALENT. BUT THEY DON'T WIN THE CUP. IT WAS THE ABILITY TO GET EVERYONE TO PLAY TOGETHER FOR EACH OTHER. AND EVERYONE CONTRIBUTED."

– BOBBY CLARKE

And Professor Shero's most constant sermon was this: Play as a team.

While the media constantly harped on the Flyers' pugilistic tendencies, the Flyers knew behind closed doors their ability to click both on and off the ice was the main reason for their success.

A SANDWICH-AND-BEER JOINT NAMED REXY'S IN SOUTH JERSEY BECAME THE POPULAR WATERING HOLE FOR THE PLAYERS.

"Toughness was part of it, physical fighting was a small part of it," recalled Bob Clarke, a three-time Hart Trophy winner. "We had a lot of talent – lots of teams have talent. But they don't win the Cup. It was the ability to get everyone to play together for each other. And everyone contributed."

A sandwich-and-beer joint named Rexy's in South Jersey became the popular watering hole for the players. Drop in there at 12:30 p.m. on a practice day and you might find half the team having lunch.

"I think that was a big part of it," Clarke said. "We liked each other off the ice. The older players were exceptionally tolerant of all the young guys. There was never a separation…we liked each other. We still do to this day."

After upsetting Bobby Orr and the Boston Bruins in 1974, the Flyers came into the following season with a lot of confidence. Allen had fleeced the California Golden Seals out of Reggie Leach to form the legendary LCB Line (Leach, Clarke, Bill Barber) and Philadelphia was off to the races again.

By mid-season, the Patrick Division race was over and at season's end, the Flyers had allowed only 181 goals, fewest in the NHL, riding the superb goaltending of Parent. Their 113 points put them in a tie with Buffalo and Montreal for league supremacy.

While the Flyers had firepower, Shero also incorporated role players into his system. These foot soldiers – Don Saleski, Orest Kindrachuk, Gary Dornhoefer, Terry Crisp, Bill Clement and Ross Lonsberry, among others – did a lot of the grunt work. They sacrificed a lot. It was all about playing for the team.

"Our third and fourth lines really complemented things because they were ahead of a lot of the teams in the league as far as from the checking standpoint," Barber said. "Through grit, muscle and talent, that team was right up there.

"I think it was a carryover from the year before. The guys were trying to repeat and that's a tough thing to do. I think the younger players were better players because they had gotten the experience that was needed to carry on. I don't think there was any doubt in the minds of any of the players in that dressing room in what direction we were going to go."

Plus there was always the fear factor, starting with Dave "The Hammer" Schultz and others like Andre "Moose" Dupont. These were the symptoms when an opposing player was mysteriously scratched due to the "Spectrum Flu."

Behind the scenes, Shero was sitting in that tiny closet of an office, plotting ways to put a new spin on some old hockey fundamentals.

Out of those sessions came the sayings on the message board. It was all part of his plan to make his team execute better by thinking the game through. That's how they stopped Orr in '74 and that's how they overcame Buffalo's French Connection Line of Gilbert Perreault, Rene Robert and Rick Martin in the '75 Cup final.

"He (Shero) had dedication to the game, knowledge of the game and more than anything, a respect for his athletes," Clement said. "A lot of coaches don't show respect for the players, they rule with the whip, instead of with rationale and caring for their athletes.

"Freddie was really an anomaly, an exception at that time because of the respect that he constantly displayed for this athletes. And I think it paid off for him all the time. The respect that Freddie showed kept everyone on an even keel."

As captain of the Flyers those years, Clarke worked closer to Shero than anyone. He saw the care exhibited by the coach, how he made players better by getting them to play the right way.

"I think it works for everybody," Clarke said. "Too many coaches use the power of their position to berate athletes because they try to get them to do what they want. That never works. And

Bobby Clarke's gap-toothed mug pops to mind any time one thinks of the Broad Street Bullies.

remember in those days, it was just coaches who had their own ideas. Giving players a hard time was accepted and sending players down was accepted."

Clarke spent nearly 25 years sitting in a GM's chair and knows how difficult it is to build a successful team. From his perspective, it was mostly about finding players with character rather than characters who just played.

He says the coach's job of making that personnel mesh and form a winning chemistry might be even tougher.

"In the 40 years I've been in the NHL, the hardest thing you can do is create a team, where everyone contributes to the outcome," Clarke said. "It's hard to get 20 guys thinking together, playing for each other. Freddie had done it before. He had done it in the minor leagues. He did it with us.

"Freddie came along and valued everybody on our team. Even though we had guys like Bob Kelly who didn't play nearly the minutes as myself, he gave him an important role on the team and gave him credit for that role. He helped our team. We weren't going to win because Bernie was going to stand on his head or Rick MacLeish was going to score three goals. Everybody was important to winning. Any coach like that is going to have success. Al Arbour was the same way. Everybody helped.

"And Freddie had everything on the ice organized. Most players need that. We were a group that needed organization, needed direction to pull us all together. And when he gave us that, we became a good team. We were having success and it just united everybody."

"IT WAS A SPECIAL TIME, BECAUSE WE HAD WON A STANLEY CUP AT HOME (1974) AND NOW WE WANTED TO WIN ONE ON THE ROAD."

– BILL BARBER

The Flyers swept Toronto in the first round, then survived a scare in the second when the New York Islanders, fresh off becoming just the second team in NHL history to rebound from a 3-0 deficit by overtaking Pittsburgh, came back from another 3-0 hole to force a Game 7 only to fall to the Flyers 4-1 in the series finale.

Barber says the Flyers paid attention to every detail. Owner Ed Snider invited the players' fathers and mothers to join them on the road for the games against Buffalo in the final, which was won by the Flyers in six games.

"I thought I was a better player the second time around than I was the first time because of what I had learned," Barber said. "I think we all were.

"Facing Buffalo, up 3-2, we tried to win that game in Buffalo. It was a special time, because we had won a Stanley Cup at home (1974) and now we wanted to win one on the road. That's pretty special in itself. On the road, it gave everyone a chance to have the ice to ourselves after all the people were on the ice the first year. Mr. Snider was nice enough to invite the moms and dads in, what a special time that was. That's something I will never forget and to this day I still thank him for that."

No. 8

2001-02 DETROIT RED WINGS

The Detroit Red Wings spanked their rivals, the Colorado Avalanche, 7–0 in Game 7 of the West final before cruising past the Carolina Hurricanes in the Stanley Cup.

BRENDAN SHANAHAN PERFECTLY exemplifies the dichotomy between two tremendous Detroit Red Wings teams.

Shanahan had a golden touch, the kind of silk hands that allow a man to score 656 career goals. But he also knew how to dent more than twine, displaying a toughness that – in combination with his skill – made him one of the best power forwards of his era.

He's also an intelligent person who can contribute articulate, insightful thoughts when called for. Conversely, when it comes to something like comparing the Red Wings teams he played for that first won the Cup in 1997, then ultimately won a third championship five years later with a star-studded cast in 2002, Shanahan is more than capable of offering an analogy that could only have come straight from a dressing room.

"The '02 team is probably the best and deepest," he said when asked to compare the top-flight Wings clubs he played on. "But in a seven-game series I think the '97 team would kick the (crap) out of the '02 team.

"I think if the '02 team played the '97 team, they better win in (Game) 4 or 5 because I think they would have limped into 7."

Then again, if the '02 edition had to rely on a little craftiness to get by in that hypothetical showdown, there's ample reason to believe they'd have sufficient supplies. Four players from that team – Steve Yzerman, Brett Hull, Luc Robitaille and Igor Larionov – are already in the Hall of Fame. Coach Scotty Bowman and owner Mike Ilitch are also in as builders.

Five more skaters – Shanahan, Chris Chelios, Sergei Fedorov, Dominik Hasek and Nicklas Lidstrom – are somewhere between locks and very good bets to get in, to say nothing of a rookie on that team named Pavel Datsyuk.

With an average age of 32.5 and eight players over 35, the Wings became the oldest team ever to win the Cup and Ilitch footed a nearly $70-million bill for the privilege of gathering such a grand array of skill.

HE ALSO KNEW HOW TO DENT MORE THAN TWINE, DISPLAYING A TOUGHNESS THAT – IN COMBINATION WITH HIS SKILL – MADE HIM ONE OF THE BEST POWER FORWARDS OF HIS ERA.

Sometimes numbers don't tell the whole story; other times, they perfectly illustrate what it was like for opponents to face a squad so formidable that games often began to swing before the opening faceoff.

"We'd come out on the ice for warmup and after the first couple laps we'd notice the other team stretching near the red line or blueline and they were all staring at us," Shanahan said. "Someone said, 'Every time we play it's 1-0 after the first three laps of warmup'."

And it wasn't just opponents who felt the glare. The big question in Detroit to start the season was how there was going to be enough room in Joe Louis Arena to house everybody's ego after an off-season in which the Wings added Dominik Hasek,

Brett Hull and Luc Robitaille to a lineup that already had its share of stars.

According to Shanahan, the presence of all those great players created a virtuous cycle that kept the greed in check.

"You get out there on the power play and the other team chips it out after a minute and you want to stay on and get that goal, but you look over at the bench and Hull, Robitaille and Yzerman have one leg over the boards, so you say, 'OK, that was my minute; they get a minute, too,' " he laughed. "And we all did that."

What's more, nobody was about to start pulling a prima donna act with Bowman behind the bench. The legendary jut-jawed coach walked away from his craft for good after the '02 triumph, which gave him an all-time record nine career Stanley Cups, one more than renowned Montreal Canadiens coach Toe Blake.

"He always kept us off-balance and, on a team of stars, probably our biggest star was the coach," Shanahan said. "We had a coach that was already in the Hall of Fame. It might be tough for somebody else to coach that group. He wasn't intimidated by us and he could coach us. He wasn't afraid to tell a 600-goal scorer he had to take shorter shifts or backcheck because he's coached Mario Lemieux, he's coached Guy Lafleur. He's happy to have us on his team, but he's not in awe of any of us."

Of the three championship Red Wings teams from '97 to '02, the final outfit had the best regular season winning percentage, a .707 mark compared to .628 in '98 and .573 in '97.

The '02 team basically went wire-to-wire in winning the Presidents' Trophy, finishing with 116 points, 15 more than second-place Boston.

They also sent a league-high 10 players to the Salt Lake City Olympics, where Yzerman sustained a knee injury that kept him out of all but one regular season contest between the end of the Games and the playoffs. His hobbling, gutsy post-season performance was a big part of what willed Detroit through the tough road to the Cup, which culminated with a five-game win over the upstart Carolina Hurricanes in the final.

Another significant aspect was the steady play of Lidstrom, who became the first European ever to claim the Conn Smythe Trophy. Shortly thereafter, Lidstrom won his second Norris Trophy, with Chelios, already 40, finishing second in the voting.

Stunning as that collection of future Hall of Famers was, the '97 squad will always hold a special spot in Shanahan's heart, not to mention the memories of Motor City fans who had been scarred by a series of bitter playoff disappointments that featured shocking first round exits in '93 and '94, a four-game sweep by the Devils in the '95 final and a six-game loss to the Colorado Avalanche in the '96 Western Conference showdown.

Shanahan joined the Wings from the Hartford Whalers at the beginning of the 1996-97 campaign, coming over in a trade he requested, in exchange for a package featuring Paul Coffey and Keith Primeau.

Most recall the championship-winning Detroit squads as teams built on finesse, highlighted by the wizardry of Russian players like Fedorov, Larionov and Viacheslav Fetisov.

Shanahan tells a much different story. "I always tell people when they ask about the Detroit teams, the '96-97 team was one of the meanest and toughest hockey teams I ever played on," he said. "We could go up against anyone in a dirty, tough hockey game.

"When we played in the playoffs in '97, a few of us would identify a key defenseman or key player on the other team and our goal was either to get him to quit the series or to knock him out of the series…that was a very mean, tough team."

The words 'mean and tough' were being tossed about all over the place on the eve of the '97 final – just not in reference to Detroit. Eric Lindros had just led the Philadelphia Flyers past Mark Messier and the New York Rangers in the East and at 24, 'The Big E' looked destined to take his place among the game's greats.

Combine a sense of Philly destiny with the fact Detroit had wilted so many times with the chips down in years past and it was clear to see why many anticipated the Flyers would chew through the Wings, extending a miserable stretch that had seen Motown go without a championship since 1955, the longest drought in the NHL.

"We were being told by everyone in the world it was Eric's time and they were big and bad," Shanahan said. "They said he basically just manhandled Messier and the Rangers and they were going to kick the (crap) out of us. I think there was a small amount of fear on our part of, 'What if everyone's right?' "

Dominik Hasek, a six-time Vezina Trophy winner, won his first of two Stanley Cups with the Red Wings in 2001–02.

They weren't. And, according to Shanahan, it didn't take long for the Wings themselves to reach that conclusion while opening the series in Philadelphia.

"I think we knew in the first three minutes of Game 1 that we were going to kick their ass," he said.

Detroit went on to sweep the Flyers and, fittingly, grinder Darren McCarty scored the series-winner by turning defenseman Janne Niinimaa inside out, before doing the same to goalie Ron Hextall. In addition to McCarty, Red ruffians like Joey Kocur, Kirk Maltby and blueliner Bob Rouse all helped set the tone.

Then there was Vladimir Konstantinov, the Russian ball of nasty who patrolled the blueline with unparalleled vitriol. Six days after the Cup triumph, Konstantinov's life changed forever when he was involved in a limousine accident that marred the Wings' celebration. Shanahan fondly recalled the role played by a man known to many simply as 'Bad Vlad.'

"Vladdy, you didn't even talk to him, you just knew he was going to do it and he was going to do it at the best and worst times," Shanahan said of Konstantinov's prickly approach. "We would be beating a team 6-0 in the regular season in a nothing game with no hits with 30 seconds to go, everyone just wants to get out of there and get on the plane and all of a sudden Vladdy would step up and hit their star player at center ice and knock him out cold.

"The last 25 seconds of the game would take 45 minutes to play.

"We'd all be in the dressing room after like, 'Thanks, Vladdy; glad I'm icing my knuckles instead of drinking the beer'."

No. 9

1991-92 PITTSBURGH PENGUINS

Jaromir Jagr and Mario Lemieux combined for 200 points in the 1991–92 regular season and another 58 in the playoffs.

ON ITS MAY 8, 1992 FRONT COVER, THE HOCKEY NEWS featured an image of a pensive-looking Mario Lemieux accompanied by a bold sell line:

NHL Dynasties, Now Dinosaurs
Dominant Teams Have Become Extinct

The statement was meant to reflect hockey's pending pendulum shift, one that would come to fruition with the Pittsburgh Penguins imminent demise. Trailing 3-1 in the first round of the playoffs to Washington, the Pens were done 'fer and it seemed a certainty we'd have our fourth different champion in four years. This after three franchises – Montreal, Edmonton and the Islanders – owned the Stanley Cup for most of the 1970s and '80s.

As history revealed, at least in 1992, it was impossible to kill a walking bird.

A season in which frequent turmoil was the underlying theme for the Pens was punctuated by an NHL record-tying 11-game post-season winning streak en route to back-to-back crowns. The champs proved the disbelievers wrong, overcoming contract squabbles, critical injuries and, most significantly, the tragic death of their coach, to reach the pinnacle.

"THAT'S THE WAY HE ALWAYS PLAYED. HE WAS A FIGHTER, AND I DON'T MEAN IN THE SENSE OF DROPPING HIS GLOVES. HE JUST NEVER GAVE UP."
– RON FRANCIS ON RICK TOCCHET

The secrets to their success? Dazzling depth, top-end talent and fierce desire.

"We had spectacular players," said TSN's Pierre McGuire, an assistant coach with the '91-92 club. "It's scary in terms of what it would cost to keep that team together today."

The depth chart is an honor roll, chock full of perennial all-stars, Hall of Famers, soon-to-be Hall of Famers and at least one should-be Hall of Famer. Start in the middle, with the best player in the league that season, Lemieux, followed by an in-his-prime Ron Francis. The checking-line/No. 3 center was Bryan Trottier. No, that's not a typo. On right wing, 40-goal man Joey Mullen was followed by Mark Recchi (then later in the season Rick Tocchet), while sophomore Jaromir Jagr was flashing signs of his burgeoning brilliance amid a 32-goal year. Left winger Kevin Stevens recorded a team-best 54 goals and 254 penalty minutes, giving Pittsburgh the pre-eminent power forward in hockey.

The blueline corps wasn't quite as star-studded, but still featured the likes of Paul Coffey (until February), Larry Murphy and Ulf and Kjell Samuelsson. And the last line of defense was money netminder Tom Barrasso.

Of the group, six – Lemieux, Francis, Trottier, Mullen, Coffey and Murphy – are already honored members of the Hall. Jagr will make it seven three years after he retires. Recchi may be a long shot, but could make it eight. Then there's Barrasso, who on merit should be a definite No. 8, or 9, but remains on the outside looking in, largely due to his prickly relationship with the media.

Gritty role players such as Bob Errey, Phil Bourque and Gordie Roberts completed a stellar mix that was ultimately coached by legend Scotty Bowman.

Beyond the talent, the club was also laden with leadership.

"Mario was the captain, but the team probably had nine captains," said Penguins vice-president Tom McMillan, who covered the team for the *Post-Gazette* in '91-92. "And you had Bryan Trottier, who completely accepted a secondary role. Completely."

Yet, despite its embarrassment of riches, this unit stumbled at times, on occasion badly. About three-quarters of the way through the season, there was still concern they might not even make the playoffs of the then 22-team league.

"WE HAD SPECTACULAR PLAYERS. IT'S SCARY IN TERMS OF WHAT IT WOULD COST TO KEEP THAT TEAM TOGETHER TODAY."

– PIERRE MCGUIRE, PENGUINS ASSISTANT COACH

"After coming off the first Cup and with (coach) Bob Johnson's illness, it seemed the whole season, we struggled along, plodded along," Murphy said. "We never really got our footing."

The tone for turmoil was set in training camp when it was learned Johnson had been diagnosed with brain cancer. 'Badger' was a universally beloved hockey man and news of his illness weighed heavily on the group. He eventually succumbed to his disease on Nov. 26, 1991.

"Everybody loved Bob," Murphy said. "It wasn't the best environment to go out there and play well. We tried to do the best under the circumstances."

Simultaneously, GM Craig Patrick had to deal with some thorny contract issues, most notably Francis, who missed nearly the entire first month of the campaign while sorting out terms of his new pact.

Fortunately for Patrick, he didn't have to turn far for a new coach; Bowman had been hired as director of player personnel in 1990 and agreed to step into the breach. Still, the transition from the affable Johnson to the my-way-or-the-highway Bowman proved challenging for some of the players – at first.

"Scotty didn't really change anything," Murphy said. "His approach was the same in terms of how we were going to play the game. Now, personality-wise, it was different. Bob Johnson was 'Mr. Bright;' 'Great Day for Hockey.' Scotty's approach wasn't as…enthusiastic. But Scotty was a great coach. We were fortunate someone like that could step in that circumstance. It wasn't easy."

It was downright dreary at first. Pittsburgh got off to a 5-6-3 start and by late February was still just .500, in a battle for the final Patrick Division playoff berth. Lemieux's notorious bad back flared frequently, limiting him to 64 games. At times, it was so painful for Lemieux, he couldn't bend over to tie his skates; instead the Penguins hired a youngster for the task. Remarkably, he still managed to win the Art Ross with 131 points.

Bowman, meanwhile, had some points to make of his own. In an attempt to rattle some cages at a practice just prior to Christmas, he delivered reassurance about his faith in the team – in the form of a veiled threat.

"He said, in the way only Scotty could say it, 'Fellas, we're going to win the Cup again, but some of you are playing as though you don't belong here,' " McGuire recalled. "'Don't be the guy who, when we're winning the Cup in June, is sitting on his couch watching us carry it around. Don't be the guy who forces us to trade you out of town to help us get better.' He got everybody's attention."

As Bowman was working his brilliance, Patrick was working the phone lines, masterminding a bold swap that catalyzed a character shift in the team's dressing room. On Feb. 19, 1992, Patrick sent Mark Recchi, Brian Benning (acquired earlier that day from Los Angeles) and a first round pick to Philadelphia for Tocchet, Kjell Samuelsson, back-up goalie Ken Wregget and a third round pick.

Of the three newcomers, Tocchet had the biggest impact. He scored, he hit, he fought – he did whatever was necessary to win and inspired teammates to soar higher and strut with a little more swagger.

The Scarborough, Ont., native was at the heart of a pivotal moment when, on March 15 in Chicago, he took a puck to the face and suffered a broken jaw. Stunningly, he returned to the contest with a spaceman-style helmet, scored two goals and opened a bunch of eyes.

"That was a bellwether moment for our group," McGuire said. "It showed you the value of Tocchet. It showed you the toughness of Tocchet and the guys started to say, 'We can get this done.' "

Added Francis: "I wouldn't expect anything less from him. That's the way he always played. He was a fighter, and I don't mean in the sense of dropping his gloves. He just never gave up."

Following a 10-day players' strike at the beginning of April, the Penguins secured third place in the division and drew the Capitals in Round 1; it was the start of a playoff trek that was a microcosm of their season.

They fell behind in the series 3-1 and were headed to Washington for Game 5. Looking like they were a dinosaur bound for extinction, Bowman decided it was time to alter strategy, eschewing the aggressive 2-1-2 forecheck for a passive 1-4 set-up. He floated the concept by Lemieux and asked his captain to sell it to some of the team's leaders. The move paid off as the Pens became much more responsible defensively and staged a dramatic comeback to win the series in seven.

Francis said Bowman also weaved wizardry in-game, managing the bench like a champion chess player.

"WE HUNG IN THERE AND AFTER THE FIRST COUPLE ROUNDS OF THE PLAY-OFFS, IT WAS LIKE WE WERE NEVER GOING TO LOSE ANOTHER GAME."

– LARRY MURPHY

"That was one of the most masterful coaching jobs I've ever seen in terms of getting the matchups he wanted," Francis said.

Round 2 against the Rangers featured another memorable come-from-behind clash. Down 2-1 and having lost Lemieux to a broken wrist – courtesy of an Adam Graves slash – and Mullen to a knee injury in the same game, the Pens needed to swing momentum.

The Rangers, who'd finished first overall, looked poised to take a 3-1 series stranglehold back to Madison Square Garden,

In addition to the Stanley Cup, the second of his career, Mario Lemieux took home the Art Ross and Conn Smythe Trophies in 1992.

holding a 4-2 lead late in Game 4. But, after the Pens killed a five-minute major midway through the third period, Francis fired an innocent-looking 60-foot slap shot at Rangers stopper Mike Richter. It found the back of the net and turned the tide in the series and the playoffs. Troy Loney tied the game a minute later and Francis won it in overtime.

"I think if I take that shot 999 times, it maybe goes in once," Francis said.

Added Murphy: "We hung in there and after the first couple rounds of the playoffs, it was like we were never going to lose another game."

They didn't. Game 4 against the Blueshirts was the first of 11 consecutive triumphs, as Pittsburgh steamrolled Boston in the conference final and Chicago in the Stanley Cup to give the Steel City its second NHL title.

Lemieux, who returned for Round 3 and finished with a league-best 16 goals and 34 points in 15 playoff games, won the Conn Smythe as playoff MVP. But Super Mario said at the time he believed it just as easily could have gone to a teammate.

"Tom Barrasso was just superb," Lemieux said. "He was the key to us winning the Cup."

Said Francis of Barrasso: "He never really got the credit he deserved. I think a lot of that has to do with the fact we were such an offensive team. We'd win games 7-6 and he didn't get much support.

"In Game 3 of the final in Chicago, we got kind of a lucky goal early, Kevin Stevens off a faceoff, and the puck was in our end pretty much the rest of the game. We ended up winning 1-0."

While Barrasso and Lemieux shone during the post-season, it was the Penguins' ability to win virtually any style of game that helped set them apart. They didn't have to rely solely on offense, defense, grit or goaltending – they had it all.

"That team could seriously beat you any way," McMillan said. "They could play a tough game, they could fight, they could play a defensive game and they could blow your doors off."

And they could win back-to-back Stanley Cups, despite The Hockey News' premature notice of extinction.

No. 10

1962-63 TORONTO MAPLE LEAFS

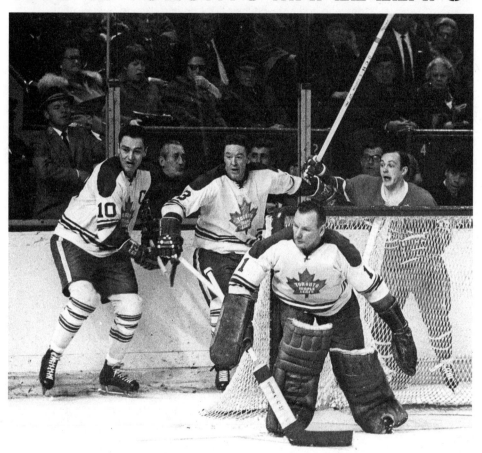

IF YOU WERE LOOKING FOR A HOCKEY TEAM that employed future Hall of Fame players at every position – and more importantly, got crucial contributions from the top of the lineup to its bottom – the 1962-63 Toronto Maple Leafs would represent your ideal choice.

Johnny Bower allowed only 10 goals in five games in the 1962–63 final against the Red Wings.

"We were mostly an older team, but we had some younger guys who could play, too – and I was one of the young guys," said Hall of Famer Dick Duff more than 47 years after that '62-63 Maple Leafs team won the organization's 11th Stanley Cup.

"We didn't play well at times during the season, but we knew what was at stake in the playoffs and the guys came together so well and took care of business. Everybody stepped up at different times...and that's what makes good teams great."

The Leafs kicked off the '62-63 campaign as defending champions who had just won their first Cup in a decade. And most of the components from that team – including captain George Armstrong, coach-GM Punch Imlach, leading scorer Frank Mahovlich and starting goalie Johnny Bower – were back in Blue and White.

In Imlach's estimation, the Cup victory should've only made that '62-63 team even more dangerous.

AFTER THEY'D BEATEN CHICAGO EARLY IN THE YEAR, A PLANE CARRYING THE LEAFS HOME WAS STRUCK BY LIGHTNING, BUT THE FLIGHT CONTINUED ON AND CONCLUDED SAFELY.

"Now they've got confidence because they know they're the best," Imlach said in the fall of 1962. "It's up to the other (teams) to come up to our level and knock us off."

Knocking off that Leafs squad required an impossible amount of knocking.

In fact – in what looked like an early warning to the NHL's other five teams – not even Mother Nature herself could've derailed Toronto that season: After they'd beaten Chicago early in the year, a plane carrying the Leafs home was struck by lightning, but the flight continued on and concluded safely.

The business angle of the game also threw a few wrenches Toronto's way. Mahovlich, center Billy Harris and veteran defensemen Red Kelly and Allan Stanley all were contract holdouts who signed with the team just prior to the signing deadline.

Once they agreed to new, improved salaries – and once other key Maple Leafs were given raises – Toronto wound up with the highest payroll in the league. The Leafs also were tied with Detroit as the NHL's oldest team (28.2 years) – and big money plus big accomplishments equaled big things were expected of them.

The problem was, the Leafs began the season looking anything but experienced and confident. And the pressure they faced necessitated rapid change.

Once Toronto lost four of its first eight games and six of its first 11, Imlach benched Bower (then a 38-year-old who in the previous three seasons with Toronto had won 98 games and his first Cup). However, by November, new starter Don Simmons was felled by the flu and Imlach worked Bower back into the mix in a platoon system once both goalies were healthy.

But, according to one ex-Leaf who retired after winning a championship with the team in 1962, Toronto's talent level made their netminding decisions almost an afterthought.

"(The) Leafs have such a good club, it shouldn't matter who plays goal," said future Hall of Famer Bert Olmstead at the time. "With three well-balanced lines and two good defense pairs and excellent reserves, they shouldn't give the opposition enough good scoring chances to cause their goalie any worry."

Up front, Toronto had all sorts of veteran warriors: Mahovlich (a nine-time 30-plus goal-scoring left winger who would chip in 36 for the Leafs in '62-63); Armstrong (who Imlach had said was washed up a year earlier, yet was still a formidable two-way center); left winger Bob Pulford (who scored at least 17 goals in 10 of his 14 seasons with Toronto); and center Ron Stewart (who represented the Leafs in four NHL All-Star Games).

Right winger Bob Nevin was only 24 and playing his third NHL season. Eddie Shack was a 25-year-old left winger who the fans adored for his on-and-off-ice rambunctious enthusiasm.

Best of all, center Dave Keon was an emerging superstar who hadn't celebrated his 23rd birthday before the season began.

"If I had to pick one out of my men, it would be Keon," Imlach said in February of 1963 when asked to identify Toronto's most important player. "I made that statement before the season began and what's happened since then makes me more positive about it. He's our best man, the top center in the National Hockey League and the most consistent player in the business."

The Leafs' situation on defense was just as impressive.

Thirty-five-year-old Kelly – a former Norris and Lady Byng Trophy winner who also was a federal politician in Canada's national parliament at the time – anchored the blueline corps. Behind him was 32-year-old perennial all-star and ferocious ironman Tim Horton.

IT WAS THE FIRST TIME IN 15 YEARS THE LEAFS HAD WON THE PRINCE OF WALES TROPHY AS TOP TEAM IN THE LEAGUE

Stanley was a 36-year-old stay-at-home defenseman who played for each of Toronto's last four Cup-winning teams; 24-year-old Carl Brewer had a breakout year in '62-63 and was named to the league's first all-star team; and Kent Douglas was a 26-year-old rookie D-man who won the Calder Trophy that season.

"We had so many good defensemen, we were able to continue on playing well even though we'd lost Bobby Baun for a while there," Duff said, referring to the Leafs legend who was out of Toronto's lineup from December to February with strained knee ligaments. "I mean, we missed Bobby, but everybody knew their role and that made it easier on the team as a whole."

The Buds coach recognized it at the time, too.

"You'd never know our defense was the best by looking at the goals-against statistics, but they can be the best any time they want to work at it," said Imlach in '62. "Douglas, for example, has been our steadiest defenseman…Horton is the best defensively…(and) Brewer carries the puck better than any defenseman we've got."

Toronto's all-around depth helped the Leafs correct their sluggish start. The Leafs were the NHL's hottest team before Christmas, with eight wins and three ties in 13 games. They also led the league in goals through the first 28 games (93 goals, including 17 from Mahovlich).

Unfortunately for the players, the iron-fisted Imlach wasn't completely satisfied. Especially when he was comparing his Leafs to Gordie Howe's imposing Red Wings.

"They keep winning the big games," Imlach said of Detroit. "What they've got over us is the fact they can beat the poor teams. We can't. Every time we get a chance to look like a big club, we blow a game to some tail-end team."

However, with the steady scoring touch of Mahovlich – who's 36 goals put him two behind Howe for the league lead – Toronto fought off Chicago down the stretch and edged out the Blackhawks by one point to finish first with a 35-23-12 record.

It was the first time in 15 years the Leafs had won the Prince of Wales Trophy as top team in the league, but it didn't help them avoid a first round playoff showdown with their archrivals from Montreal.

The Leafs also had added incentive when the league announced the payout to the Cup-winning team would rise to $63,000 ($36,000 for a Cup win and $27,000 for an opening round series win).

That meant the payout to each player on a Cup champion would be $3,600.

"That was nothing to sneeze at back then," Duff said with a laugh. "We wanted to win, anyway, but that didn't hurt the cause."

Toronto's focus was on display immediately against Montreal. The Leafs won the first three games of the series, leaning heavily on Bower (who stopped 80 of 83 shots in those games) and the aforementioned spread-out attack on offense.

The Canadiens won Game 4 by a score of 3-1, but the Leafs stormed back in Game 5 and dominated in a 5-0 victory that saw Bower stop all 35 shots.

Toronto's win over the Habs set up a Cup final against the Red Wings that served as a rubber match of sorts between the two franchises. The Leafs and Detroit had met 18 times in the play-offs prior to 1963 – and both teams had won nine series apiece.

But Toronto got on track very early in the final – thanks to Duff's two goals in Game 1, which established a record for fastest two goals to start a game by a single player (68 seconds) – and the Leafs won the first battle 4-2.

In Game 2, the Leafs were without Mahovlich (who was out with a bruised knee), but little-used forward Eddie Litzenberger – a former Red Wing who was released by Detroit in 1961 – scored a goal and assisted on two others for another 4-2 win for Toronto.

Former Leaf Alex Faulkner scored midway through the second period of Game 3 to secure a 3-2 victory for Detroit. But Kelly and Keon combined for three goals and four points for Toronto in Game 4 (a 4-2 Leafs win) – and in Game 5, Keon opened the scoring and Shack deflected Douglas' shot for the Cup-winning goal in Toronto's 3-1 series clincher.

When it was over, Imlach made clear who his best player was.

"I'd have to take Davey (Keon)," Imlach said when asked to pick a playoff MVP. "It may sound like a lot of big talk, but I wouldn't trade him for Gordie Howe."

"THAT WAS NOTHING TO SNEEZE AT BACK THEN. WE WANTED TO WIN, ANYWAY, BUT THAT DIDN'T HURT THE CAUSE."

– DICK DUFF ON THE $3,600 BONUS EACH PLAYER EARNED FOR WINNING THE STANLEY CUP

Tim Horton won four
Stanley Cups and was
inducted into the
Hockey Hall of Fame in
1977.

No. 11

1968-69 MONTREAL CANADIENS

Serge Savard won eight Stanley Cups with the Montreal Canadiens and was inducted into the Hall of Fame in 1986.

IN HIS 14 YEARS AS GM OF THE MONTREAL CANADIENS, Sam Pollock guided the team to a remarkable nine Stanley Cups. He is the only executive in NHL history to lead his teams to Stanley Cups in both the pre- and post-expansion eras. He did it by having unfettered access to the best players in the province of Quebec and later, when the playing field was leveled, with the NHL draft. He did it in his first season as a GM and again in his last.

He assembled what some believe to be the greatest dynasty of all-time, the Canadiens team that won four consecutive Stanley Cups in the late 1970s. But Pollock always had a fondness for the Habs teams of the late '60s, a group that won four Stanley Cups in five seasons and is often referred to as, "The Forgotten Dynasty."

"I don't really understand why everybody is so anxious to compare the Montreal Canadiens of the 1950s with the team of the late '70s," Pollock once said. "There was a team in the middle that might have been as good."

Pollock is right. The team that won Stanley Cups in 1965, '66, '68 and '69 is not celebrated the way the other dynasties were, but perhaps it should be. The reason it's not remembered is the fact those four teams, of which the 1968-69 version was the best, were a triumph of the collective in a city and organization that had always had some of the most dynamic superstars in the game. The best any player ever finished in the scoring race was tied for second.

And the '68-69 Habs epitomized that concept. While Serge Savard became the first defenseman in NHL history to win the Conn Smythe Trophy as most valuable player of the playoffs, not a single Montreal player won an individual award for his regular season performance. With 43 goals and 87 points, Yvan Cournoyer led the team in scoring, but was just sixth in the league and only Jean Beliveau joined him in the top 10 scorers.

"I WAS SURPRISED WHEN THEY GOT ME BE-CAUSE THAT WAS THE LAST PLACE I EVER THOUGHT I WOULD BE ABLE TO PLAY. MONTREAL, CRIPES, THEY WERE ALWAYS GREAT. WHEN THEY TRADED FOR ME, IT WAS A DREAM COME TRUE."

– TED HARRIS

Not one Canadiens player made the first all-star team, with the honors going to Glenn Hall of the St. Louis Blues in goal, Bobby Orr of the Boston Bruins and Tim Horton of the Toronto Maple Leafs on defense, Phil Esposito of the Bruins at center, Bobby Hull of the Chicago Black Hawks at left wing and Gordie Howe of the Detroit Red Wings at right wing.

But that didn't stop the Habs, who were seven points behind the Bruins midway through the season, from establishing an NHL record for wins with 46, which was one better than the 1955-56 Canadiens. They also amassed 103 points, which was two better than the 1950-51 Red Wings.

"When you look back at it now, it was a bunch of throw-togeth-ers as far as I was concerned," said defenseman Ted Harris, who came over from American League Springfield in the summer of

'63 and stayed until 1970. "I was surprised when they got me because that was the last place I ever thought I would be able to play. Montreal, cripes, they were always great. When they traded for me, it was a dream come true."

But it would be gilding the lily just a little to suggest Montreal was a band of ragamuffins that willed its way to a championship. The '68-69 team had 10 future Hall of Famers play at least one game for them that season, including Cournoyer, Savard and Jacques Lemaire, who were all under 25 at the time. Jacques Laperriere was 27 and the Habs had a 20-year-old named Guy Lapointe, who appeared in one game.

Goalie Tony Esposito, who would later make his way to the Hall of Fame, played 13 games that season and none in the playoffs. With Gump Worsley and Rogie Vachon ahead of him on the depth chart, Esposito was claimed by the Black Hawks in the intraleague draft that summer. That's how good the Canadiens were.

Worsley and Vachon shared the bulk of the goaltending duties during the season and Vachon took over midway through the playoffs when Worsley was knocked out with a broken finger. Vachon went 7-1 for Montreal in the post-season and was brilliant at times. He posted a 1.42 goals-against average and after being called a Jr. B goalie by Toronto Maple Leafs coach-GM Punch Imlach prior to the 1967 final – which the Habs lost – it was a matter of sweet redemption for Vachon.

"It's the old story about when a guy gets hot," Harris said, "And Rogie was hot, there was no doubt about that."

Rogie Vachon sparkled in the 1968–69 playoffs going 7–1 with a 1.42 GAA.

Just how stacked was Montreal at the time? Consider all three finalists for the 1969 Calder Trophy as the NHL's top rookie were

members of the Canadiens organization the season before. Danny Grant, who won the award, had been dealt to the Minnesota North Stars in the summer of 1968, as had runner-up Norm Ferguson to the Oakland Golden Seals. Third-place finisher Gerry Desjardins, had been traded to the Los Angeles Kings during the off-season in 1968 for two first round picks, one of which was used to select future Hall of Famer Steve Shutt in 1972.

"I DON'T REALLY UNDERSTAND WHY EVERYBODY IS SO ANXIOUS TO COMPARE THE MONTREAL CANADIENS OF THE 1950S WITH THE TEAM OF THE LATE '70S. THERE WAS A TEAM IN THE MIDDLE THAT MIGHT HAVE BEEN AS GOOD."

– SAM POLLOCK

"It was unbelievable that a guy like Grant had to leave," Harris said, "because he was one heck of a hockey player."

That season also marked John Ferguson's career high for penalty minutes with 185. While the Canadiens had more than their share of talent, they also possessed toughness by the ton, thanks in large part to Ferguson and Harris, who was the designated tough guy on the blueline and racked up 102 PIM himself that season.

"They needed some grunts back there," Harris said. "They had some damn good goal-scorers. Jean Beliveau made the damn game look so easy."

The times were changing and the fact the Habs were able to change with them made their accomplishments that much more impressive. The league had instituted its first true amateur draft in 1969 and while the Canadiens still had the top two picks in that inaugural event, their luxury of cherry picking the best players in their home province had come to an end. The league had doubled in size by that time and the Habs had to deal with the retirement of coach Toe Blake after winning the Cup in 1968.

Claude Ruel took over behind the bench and despite being forced to replace a legend, managed to win the Stanley Cup in his rookie season after his team defeated the St. Louis Blues, coached by Scotty Bowman, in four straight games in the final.

Ruel's tenure as bench boss in Montreal was short, but he was a very good coach. His legacy with the Habs was built more in his ability to spot talent for Pollock where nobody else could, as evidenced by the fact Montreal drafted both Larry Robinson and Bob Gainey when he was director of scouting.

"The players listened to him and they played for him," Harris said. "Some of the guys like Savard used to really give him a hard time, but it was all in good fun."

What also made the Canadiens' run impressive was they were able to overtake and hold off the Bruins, a team that was on the rise to being a Stanley Cup contender. Phil Esposito won the scoring championship and took home the Hart Trophy as MVP, and Bobby Orr had won the second of his eight straight Norris Trophies and was on the verge of becoming a superstar. That season, he had broken Flash Hollett's 24-year-old record for goals by a defenseman, with 21.

The Canadiens ended up defeating the Bruins in the second-last game of that season to secure the NHL record for wins and points, then went on to upend the Bruins in six games in the semifinal, a playoff series many pointed to as the real Stanley Cup showdown.

As it turned out, the best team of "The Forgotten Dynasty" was its last as well. The Habs went on to miss the playoffs the next season (albeit with a 38-22-16 record), then went on their run of six Stanley Cups in the 1970s. But the 1969 Cup capped an era in which Montreal established itself as the premier NHL franchise beyond a shadow of a doubt.

"This may be the last dynasty in professional sports now that the draft systems are balancing teams everywhere," observed North Stars GM Wren Blair at the time. "But it's a dynasty that may last a long time. It's going to be much harder to pull down the Canadiens than either the Yankees or the Green Bay Packers."

Blair wasn't exactly right, since the Canadiens of the 1970s pulled down the Canadiens of the 1960s quite decisively. But that should not take any luster off a team that was equally talented and workmanlike and, in the pantheon of great Montreal teams, was definitely more than the sum of its parts.

No. 12

2000-01 COLORADO AVALANCHE

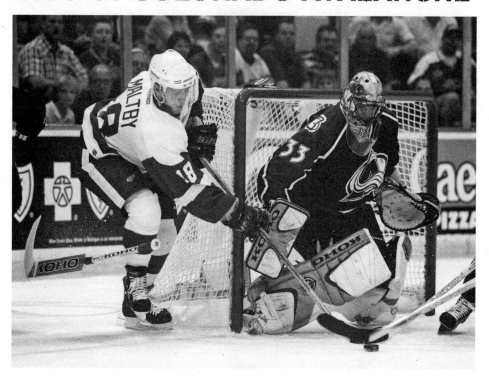

THE STAR-STUDDED 2000-01 COLORADO AVALANCHE was a team on a mission.

Following the franchise's first Stanley Cup win in its first year in Denver in 1996, the Avs were knocked out during the Conference final three of the next four years after finishing atop their division each of those seasons. In both 1999 and 2000, the stacked Avs were beaten by a similarly loaded Dallas Stars team in Game 7 of the West final, falling just short of the biggest stage.

When Ray Bourque, who the Avalanche acquired in 2000, decided to come back for one last kick at Stanley's can, it became a source of inspiration for the team to give the wily old vet an opportunity to raise the Cup for the first time. Bourque hadn't even been to a final since the 1990 Bruins lost to the Edmonton Oilers, but his years of experience spoke louder than words and

Goaltender Patrick Roy's play in the 2001 playoffs earned him the Conn Smythe Trophy, the third of his illustrious NHL career.

everybody was on board with 'Mission 16W,' a moniker derived from the 16 wins needed to take home Stanley. Even Bourque himself stitched "16W" into his baseball cap to rally the troops.

"When Ray made the decision to come back, it inspired everybody," said Hall of Fame goaltender and Cup-winning Av Patrick Roy. "From the first day, I can tell you, we were on a mission. It was clear that our goal was to win the Stanley Cup and everything was in place to do that. We had our minds set for that. Nothing was going to stop us."

Avs GM Pierre Lacroix was far from satisfied with the recent "oh-so-close" finishes. With a penchant for making cannon ball dives into the trade market, acquiring Roy in '95 and Bourque in 2000, Lacroix was a master at breaking down his assets and squeezing every last ounce of value out of them. Whether it was a first round pick or a 27-year-old Brian Rolston, Lacroix wasn't afraid of lopping off large portions of his extensive depth chart if it meant acquiring a difference-making superstar in return.

And even though this edition of the Avs began with a lineup that would make any GM salivate, Joe Sakic, Peter Forsberg, Adam Foote, Roy, Bourque and all of the team's young studs weren't enough. Lacroix was out to land the biggest fish available in 2001: Los Angeles Kings captain Rob Blake.

To be sure, it wasn't easy giving up defenseman Aaron Miller, winger Adam Deadmarsh – whose wife had just delivered twins – and a first round pick on Feb. 21, 2001, but it was a move the shrewd GM felt he owed to the fans and team to try and spare them from another devastating Game 7 loss late in the post-season.

> "WHEN RAY MADE THE DECISION TO COME BACK, IT INSPIRED EVERYBODY. FROM THE FIRST DAY, I CAN TELL YOU, WE WERE ON A MISSION."
>
> – PATRICK ROY

"We said, 'that could be the piece that's missing on this team to have one of the most balanced defense corps,' " Lacroix said. "It was the dot we missed the previous two years. We were missing something additional on the defense corps by being kicked out in Game 7. It's not easy to point out specifics when you lose in Game 7 of the Conference final in our sport, but we felt we needed to do this one in order to just give us that little edge."

And though the deep defense consisting of Bourque, Blake, Foote, Greg de Vries, Martin Skoula, Jon Klemm and Eric Messier was a daunting force, the Avs boasted a wealth of talent, young and old, up front as well. Sakic and Forsberg led the way, but it was the kids in their early-20s, Milan Hejduk, Alex Tanguay and Chris Drury, who anchored the attack. Hejduk scored 41 goals, Tanguay notched 77 points and Drury was a clutch performer with a strong two-way presence.

"The bottom line is to make sure you have Tanguay, Drury and Hejduk following the leaders," Lacroix explained. "This was the ultimate team that had the perfect mix of spices. This is the perfect team. One without the other would probably have not made it."

The whole season for the Avs played out as if it was plucked from a storybook. Roy broke Terry Sawchuk's all-time wins mark early on and the Pepsi Center played host to the 51st NHL All-Star Game in February. Pitting North America against the World, the Avalanche was represented by five players. The showcase was started in a festive fashion for Avs fans as Sakic and Forsberg faced off against each other to start the game, which North America won 14-12.

With few obstacles to overcome in the regular season, the Avs rolled along as planned. They didn't lose their first game until Oct. 30 and only went through one extended losing skid all year, dropping four in a row between Feb. 1 and 10. The team also enjoyed four separate winning streaks of at least five games, the best being a nine-game run from Oct. 10-28. And despite a comparatively weak 3-3-1 finish to the year, Colorado finished with a 52-16-14 record for 118 points, earning the franchise's second Presidents' Trophy in five years.

In the first round of the playoffs, the Avalanche faced their division rivals from Vancouver, a team Colorado was 3-2 against in the regular season and held a 28-point advantage over. Much like the point-differential suggests, the series wasn't even close. The Avs pulled off the only first round sweep in the Western Conference, closing out Vancouver's season in British Columbia with a 5-1 victory in the final game.

The Western Conference semifinal presented the Avs with their first road bump. Despite bouncing back from a Game 1 loss to take a 3-1 series lead on the seventh-seeded Los Angeles Kings – who knocked off the Detroit Red Wings 4-2 in Round 1 – the highest scoring team from the West was shutout twice in a row by Felix Potvin in consecutive 1-0 decisions.

With the series headed back to Denver for the deciding game, the veteran experience of the Avalanche came to the fore. The game entered the third period tied 1-1, even though the Avs held a distinct 23-14 shot advantage. But with three goals in eight minutes and an empty-netter at the end, Colorado came away with a 5-1 victory to advance to their third-straight West final.

"I WAS AT A RESTAURANT AFTER WE WON GAME 7 AGAINST THE KINGS AND I GOT A PHONE CALL THAT OUR DOCTOR WAS ON THE WAY TO THE HOSPITAL TO DO AN EMERGENCY SURGERY TO REMOVE PETER FORSBERG'S SPLEEN."

– GM PIERRE LACROIX

"Because we were in such control of our emotions all year it enabled us to always have the same focus and we had a lot of leadership," Roy said.

But even though the Avs were able to overcome that scare from the Kings, the team was about to face its biggest point of adversity all year, one that would leave many teams incapacitated so late in the game.

"I remember it like it was yesterday," Lacroix recalled. "I was at a restaurant after we won Game 7 against the Kings and I got a phone call that our doctor was on the way to the hospital to do an emergency surgery to remove Peter Forsberg's spleen."

One of the central pieces of Colorado's offense, Forsberg and his superb playmaking, was lost for the remainder of the season due to a freak injury. The timing couldn't have been worse for the Avs, who were suddenly being reminded of their shortcomings in recent years in the semifinal round. But what was about to be displayed against the St. Louis Blues was a lesson in leadership and depth, a seminar of what made this team so great from top to bottom.

"It would have been easy for this group to just say, 'We had a good run, we did well', but that's not what we wanted, we wanted to win," Roy recalled. "Everyone was chipping in, it didn't matter who was scoring or coming in and out of the lineup. We had guys like Dave Reid who played a big role with Shjon Podein, these guys were great leaders."

Despite the loss of Forsberg, Colorado found no trouble in dispatching the 103-point Blues in five games.

"That really shows the strength of the group," Lacroix said. "Every event of the year, every piece of adversity we had to face, there was so much leadership in that group. They had this ability, this character to turn the page on every negative thing that would happen during the year."

The Avs faced their biggest challenge yet in the Cup final against Martin Brodeur and the defending champion New Jersey Devils.

The matchup pitted the two most offensive teams from each conference against each other and also showcased two of the best goalies of their generation. Even though Colorado established the pace early with a 5-0 win in Game 1, the rest of the series was a back and forth battle.

With the series tied 2-2 heading back to the Pepsi Center for Game 5, New Jersey took its first lead of the series, scoring twice in the first period and never trailing. After posting five goals in Game 1, Colorado had only managed just seven in the next four games.

But perhaps a slice of destiny played a part in Colorado's comeback.

Heading to New Jersey for a pivotal Game 6 showdown, the Avs took the bus to Continental Airlines Arena off the New Jersey Turnpike, going the usual route that involved taking an appropriately named exit off the toll road.

"I don't remember who it was, but someone pointed out that it was Exit 16W," Lacroix said. "I couldn't believe it."

Roy once again led the way, posting his fourth shutout of the playoffs and second of the series as the Avs headed back home for a final, one-game showdown after a decisive 4-0 win.

"Going into Denver for Game 7, the fans, it was electric out there," Roy recalled. "It was a great feeling playing this game."

In another show of the team's depth and determination, the 21-year-old Tanguay scored two goals, including the game-winner, and Sakic gave the Avs a three-goal advantage in the second period to put it out of reach.

With a 1.70 goals-against average, .934 save percentage and four shutouts, Roy won his record-setting third Conn Smythe Trophy. Sakic's 54 goals and 118 regular season points earned him the Hart Trophy. And with the 3-1 Game 7 win at the Pepsi Center, 'Mission 16W' was capped off with the first championship win by a professional Colorado sports team within state lines.

SAKIC AND FORSBERG LED THE WAY, BUT IT WAS THE KIDS IN THEIR EARLY-20S, MILAN HEJDUK, ALEX TANGUAY AND CHRIS DRURY, WHO ANCHORED THE ATTACK.

And the journey was made complete when the customary awarding of the Stanley Cup to the captain was presented to Sakic. He immediately passed it off to an emotional Bourque, who finally got to elevate it over his head.

"Everyone did what they needed to do," Lacroix said. "I have a hard time describing a performance like we had that year."

No. 13

1938-39 BOSTON BRUINS

Milt Schmidt, who spent his entire 16-year NHL career with Boston, scored 15 goals and 32 points in 41 games for the 1938–39 Bruins.

A BETTING MAN OR WOMAN could have seen the Stanley Cup making a return to Boston sometime in the late 1930s.

Of course, it would have helped if they'd first hung around the Kitchener-Waterloo region of Ontario and then spent some time in Providence, R.I., after that.

That's where the seeds of the Boston Bruins' near-dynasty – four straight first-place finishes and two Cups – were sown.

Cup-less since 1929, the Bruins' first championship team had largely dissolved as the 1940s approached. Links to the past – ever-fierce defenseman Eddie Shore (although gradually absent the double-digit goal and triple-digit penalty-minute totals), goalie 'Tiny' Thompson, selfless winger-turned-blueliner Dit Clapper – were still key to Boston's present. But after their appearance in the 1930 final, the Bruins were either early-round playoff fodder (1931, '33, and '35 through '38) or failed to qualify for the post-season.

To the north and just to the south, however, help for the old guard, as well as for younger stars like Bill Cowley, was on the way.

From the Kitchener-Waterloo area came the trio known, in a day and age of political incorrectness, as the 'Kraut Line.' (While it referenced the large number of citizens of German descent in their home region, the nickname wasn't applied until the linemates had turned pro.)

Center Milt Schmidt, right winger Bobby Bauer and left winger Woody Dumart, teammates with the Ontario Hockey Association's Kitchener Greenshirts, were all signed by Boston coach-GM Art Ross (Schmidt was the last to come on, after first balking at Ross' offer of a $2,000 salary). The threesome spent much of the 1936-37 season with the International-American League's Providence Reds (where coach Albert Leduc gave the line its name) and completed their rise to the NHL by 1937-38.

With the Dumart-Schmidt-Bauer combination providing offensive support that six-time scoring-leader Cowley's line had so lacked, the Bruins finished first in the American Division in '37-38 – Boston's first No. 1 finish since 1934-35 – and led the eight-team league in wins (30) and points (67) during the 48-game season. With Shore and Clapper still at the forefront on the back end – and Thompson in usual form – Boston also allowed just 89 goals, fewest in the league.

FROM THE KITCHENER-WATERLOO AREA CAME THE TRIO KNOWN, IN A DAY AND AGE OF POLITICAL INCORRECTNESS, AS THE 'KRAUT LINE.'

The Cup didn't follow, though. Matched against Canadian Division winner Toronto in the semifinals, the Bruins were swept in three games – all of them decided by a single goal, two in overtime. Boston was outscored 6-3.

Ross began to think of what else he had stashed in Providence.

Shore had won his fourth Hart Trophy and was joined as a first all-star selection by Cowley, who finished sixth in the NHL with 39 points and had scored two of Boston's post-season goals. The B's were set there, with youngsters Bauer (20 goals as a rookie), Schmidt and Dumart (identical 13-14-27 totals), but something had to change.

Ross didn't do the unthinkable until almost a month into 1938-39 and the result was nearly unimaginable: Thompson, coming off his fourth Vezina Trophy, but now closing in on 32 years old, was traded to Detroit in late November, 1938, a night after beating the New York Americans, 8-2. The price: Norm Smith, who never played a game for the Bruins, and $15,000.

The reason: Frank Brimsek, he of a 1.75 goals-against average for Providence in '37-38 and a guy who had shown enough in Boston at the start of '38-39 when Thompson was sidelined briefly by an eye problem to make a believer of Ross.

The deal wasn't made until Boston completed a 3-0-1 homestand. It was a wise move by Ross, it turned out, because the Bruins were up in Montreal, far from their shocked, saddened fans, when the 23-year-old Brimsek (an American, of all things, from Eveleth, Minn.), lost his debut as a No. 1 goalie, 2-0.

Soon enough, though, fans couldn't wait to see him. Brimsek immediately posted three consecutive shutout victories, logging 231 minutes, 54 seconds of perfect goaltending (enough to beat Thompson's league-record 224:47) between goals. Proving that was no fluke, he reeled-off three more shutouts after the first streak was broken in a 3-2 victory over Montreal, refusing to allow a goal for 220 minutes, 24 seconds.

With six shutouts in seven games, the legend of 'Mr. Zero' was born. Another legend was in the Bruins' midst, but nobody knew that until spring.

Just before '37-38, Ross signed free agent Mel Hill and kept him in Providence for what proved to be a decent IAHL season (13 goals, 23 points in 40 games). Hill also scored two goals in eight games with Boston – enough for Ross to keep him around in a third-line role in '38-39. The Bruins didn't need Hill to score – after all, they still had Cowley (42 points), who meshed so well with rookie Roy Conacher that the freshman led the NHL with 26 goals. And they had Schmidt's line, but Hill had enough touch to turn limited ice time into 10 goals and 20 points in 44 games.

When the Bruins needed him in the playoffs, however, Hill's touch suddenly became golden. In an unexpectedly tough semi-final series with the New York Rangers (who finished 16 points behind Boston in the regular season), Hill scored a record three overtime winners – two of them ending triple-overtime marathons and the last one sending the Bruins to the finals. 'Sudden Death' Hill scored with 35 seconds left in the third overtime of Game 1; after a measly 8:24 in Game 2; and, finally, after 48 tension-filled extra minutes in Game 7 at Boston Garden.

By contrast, the five-game final against Toronto was relatively tame. The same might be said for Boston's second Cup of the era, in 1941 – except that in some ways, it was sweeter than the '39 championship that ended a 10-year drought. That's because, despite their third straight first-place finish and a league-leading 170 goals, the Bruins hadn't repeated in 1940.

It's hard to see how they didn't. Shore retired after just four games in 1939-40 to focus on becoming the player-coach-GM-owner (and, many felt, tyrant) of the IAHL's Springfield Indians; Ross had handed off the coaching reigns to Cooney Weiland, a member of Boston's first championship team, but just about everything else was in place.

Schmidt, Dumart and Bauer, now answering to the name 'The Buddy Line,' finished 1-2-3 in league scoring – Schmidt with 52 points, his wingers with 43 apiece.

"It was one of those incredible lines that had all the elements," said Kevin Shea, the Hockey Hall of Fame's editor of publications and online features. "They were tough, they were great playmakers, they had great shots and they were as good defensively as they were offensively. They were a superb force for the Bruins at the time."

Cowley had another nearly 40-point season; Conacher, despite missing 17 games, was a point-per-game player (18-12-30 in 31 games); and Boston added another 20-goal scorer in Herb Cain, whom they acquired from Montreal for mid-1930s stalwarts Charlie Sands and Ray Getliffe. Brimsek, coming off his unprecedented first season – Vezina Trophy, Calder Trophy, first-team all-star – was again virtually flawless. He didn't match the 1.57 goals-against average he posted as a rookie, but his 1.99 was no disgrace, either.

"THEY WERE TOUGH, THEY WERE GREAT PLAYMAKERS, THEY HAD GREAT SHOTS AND THEY WERE AS GOOD DEFENSIVELY AS THEY WERE OFFENSIVELY."

– KEVIN SHEA OF THE HOCKEY HALL OF FAME ON THE KRAUT LINE

The B's collapsed in the semifinals against the Rangers, though. After taking a 2-1 lead in the series, the offense dried up – one goal over the next three games – and Brimsek couldn't get the big win. The final score in Game 6 – Rangers 4, Bruins 1 – was shocking, yet motivating.

The '40-41 Bruins, while not necessarily dominant (they tied 13 games and finished second in the seven-team league with 27 wins), finished first for the fourth-straight season, at one point going unbeaten during 23-straight games – 15 wins, eight ties. Cowley led the league in scoring with 62 points (including a then-record 45 assists in 46 games) and won the Hart Trophy as league MVP. Plus, four teammates were first- or second-team all-stars. They had to overcome 2-1 and 3-2 deficits in their semifinal series against the Maple Leafs, but after advancing via consecutive 2-1 victories in Games 6 and 7, Boston went on to sweep Detroit in the final.

The Bruins' future seemed unlimited, but the Second World War took precedence. Schmidt, Dumart and Bauer were among those who dutifully registered for military service and, while they played three-quarters of the '41-42 season, were pressed into service about a month before the playoffs.

Their departure was unforgettable – 22 points between the three of them in an 8-1 victory over Montreal on Feb. 10, 1942 at Boston Garden. Following the victory, players from both teams carried the trio off the ice on their shoulders.

While they returned to resume brilliant careers in 1945-46, championships didn't come back with them. And Brimsek, who served the U.S. in 1943-44 and 1944-45, wasn't the same goal-tender when he came back.

It had been a golden age in Bruins history. No fewer than seven future Hockey Hall of Fame members – Shore and Clapper (the latter being the only player to win three Cups as a Bruin) from the first championship era; Cowley and the incoming regime of Schmidt, Bauer, Dumart and Brimsek from the '39 and '41 champions. Throw in Ross and Weiland, the Cup-winning coaches, and the number of Hall of Famers reached nine.

Except for the occasional appearance in the final in the 1950s, it would be roughly a generation before the Bruins were again considered a consistent Cup threat.

But contenders in the late '60s and early '70s had roots in the '30s and '40s. Schmidt – the only man to serve the franchise as player, captain, coach and GM – was the GM who built the Big, Bad Bruins.

THEIR DEPARTURE WAS UNFORGETTABLE – 22 POINTS BETWEEN THE THREE OF THEM IN AN 8-1 VICTORY OVER MONTREAL. FOLLOWING THE VICTORY, PLAYERS FROM BOTH TEAMS CARRIED THE TRIO OFF THE ICE ON THEIR SHOULDERS.

No. 14

1988-89 CALGARY FLAMES

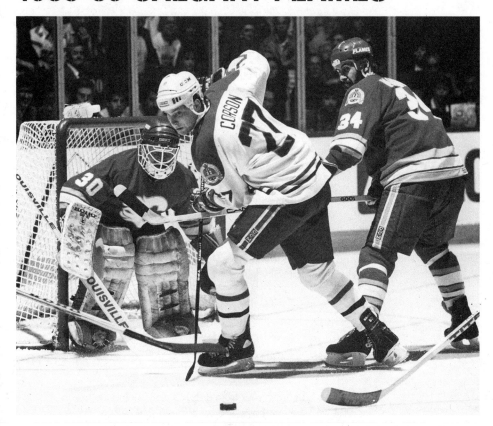

DO A YOUTUBE SEARCH for the greatest glove saves of all-time and you're bound to see a couple Mike Vernon stops from the 1988-89 season in which Calgary won the Stanley Cup.

What's most remarkable about that is they came from the same period in the seventh and deciding game of an opening round series with the Vancouver Canucks. And that period was overtime.

"I can still see that glove save he made on Tony Tanti," said Calgary Flames original and current play-by-play man Peter Maher. "I can still see it. And I can still see the one he made on (Stan Smyl)."

Flames goalie Mike Vernon lost only six times in 52 regular season games and five times in 22 playoff appearances during Calgary's Cup run in 1988–89.

Ask around and you'll hear about the other big saves he made in overtime April 15, 1989. There was one on Trevor Linden.

"I remember ones on Petri Skriko and Greg Adams, too," said center Joel Otto.

It was then Otto's destiny to get the series winner at 19:21 of overtime.

"(Hakan) Loob got it to (Jim) Peplinski wide," Otto recalled. "There was no secret to our line. Just try to get it to the net and create havoc. Luckily it went in off my foot and the rest is history."

Said Maher: "If they had a review today, it might not have counted. It went off Otto's skate into the goal. In those days, there was no review."

Good thing for the Flames. They might still be searching for their first Cup had that goal been waved off. The '88-89 Flames played as though they were a team of destiny. They led the league with 117 points on a 54-17-9 record and were first or second in the league in goals for, goals against, power play efficiency and penalty killing.

"We lost to Montreal in the 1986 final and we just assumed we'd be back every year after that," said co-captain Lanny McDonald. "By 1989, we realized if we didn't win it then, because everyone was getting a bit older, would they or could they stand to leave the team together?"

Terry Crisp had taken over from Bob Johnson behind the bench in 1987 and the emphasis was on offense, initiated by mobile puck-moving blueliners Al MacInnis and Gary Suter and executed by finishers such as 50-goal men Joe Mullen and Joe Nieuwendyk.

"That team had everything," Maher said. "The bench was solid offensively and defensively. There didn't seem to be a flaw. I talk to guys on that team now and they talk about the fourth line. That fourth line could be the No. 2 line on the current team. There was so much depth, they were able to trade a scorer like Brett Hull just to get insurance."

Hull was 23 when he broke in with the Flames in 1987-88. The right winger scored 26 goals and 50 points in 52 games as a rookie when Calgary GM Cliff Fletcher felt he needed blueline depth and a proven backup to Vernon between the pipes. So, on March 7, 1988, Fletcher dealt the future Hall of Famer to St. Louis for Rob Ramage and Rick Wamsley, a trade that looks one-sided today, but at the time was one of the final pieces to Calgary's Cup puzzle.

"THERE WAS NO SECRET TO OUR LINE. JUST TRY TO GET IT TO THE NET AND CREATE HAVOC."

– JOEL OTTO

The Calgary defense had hard-shooting MacInnis and crafty Suter running the power play, Brad McCrimmon and Jamie Macoun playing robust two-way games, and Dana Murzyn and Ric Nattress in shutdown roles. Ramage, the first overall draft pick in 1979 and 29 at the time, was an all-around defender who was versatile enough to excel in any game situation.

When Suter went down with a broken jaw in the first round, the ability of Ramage to fill his role on the power play and eat up additional minutes on the blueline proved invaluable. The Calgary defense didn't miss a beat as the playoffs wore on.

But it wasn't smooth sailing throughout for the Flames. The fact they were pushed to seven games in the opening round by a Vancouver team that finished 43 points behind them during the regular season is proof there was a lot of anxiety. Calgary lost the opener in overtime, but rebounded for wins in Games 2 and 3. After splitting the next two games, the Canucks forced Game 7 with a convincing 6-3 win in Vancouver.

"I remember getting on the bus after the post-game radio show of Game 6 and I was no sooner on than they told me to get off," Maher recalled. "They asked all the media people to leave the bus. Cliff (Fletcher) went in and they closed the door. I don't know if he ripped them or what, but he did have a sermon with them. That might have been a turning point for that team."

Otto remembers that series against Vancouver as being a confidence builder.

"The whole season was a focus for us," said Otto, now an assistant coach with the Western League's Calgary Hitmen. "Guys had a lot of personal pride during the season. As the season wore on we were fighting for first place and the Presidents' Trophy. Then the playoffs came and we knew it was now or never.

"We played a Vancouver team that had nothing to lose. They came in and played great. Whether we were gripping the sticks too tight or it was just first round jitters, I don't know. But Vancouver found a way to get that opportune goal and we ended up needing Mike to stand on his head in goal."

In the second round, the Flames had little trouble with their old nemesis, Wayne Gretzky, in his first season with the Kings. Calgary swept Los Angeles, outscoring them 22-11. The Flames then disposed of Chicago in five games in the conference final setting the stage for a re-match of the 1986 Cup final with the Canadiens, the No. 2 team during the season.

"Everything was pointing towards a Calgary-Montreal show-down," said the famously moustached McDonald, now a consultant with Baker Hughes, a Calgary oil and gas company. "We still had quite a few guys from that '86 team. But this time we just weren't willing to let each other down. We had great goaltending, phenomenal depth up front. Our three centers down the middle were Joe Nieuwendyk, Doug Gilmour and Joel Otto. Where are you going to find two better offensive guys and one better checker in the middle?"

Nieuwendyk, then 22 and already a two-time 50-goal scorer, centered 22-year-old Gary Roberts and Loob. The second line consisted of Gilmour between Joe Mullen and Colin Patterson. Mullen led playoff goal-scorers that spring with 16 in 21 games. Otto, a hulking shutdown specialist, also contributed offense with 53 points that season and 19 in 22 playoff games. He played with a variety of wingers, including McDonald, Peplinski, Mark Hunter and Jiri Hrdina. The fourth line consisted of late-season acquisition Brian MacLellan with enforcer Tim Hunter and 20-year-old mid-season call-up Theoren Fleury.

"The Flames lost three games in a row in December and called up Fleury from Salt Lake in the IHL," Maher recalled. "After that, they never had a losing streak of significance. Not to say Fleury was a huge difference-maker, he just added to their great depth."

"WHEN HE FIRST CAME IN, HE COULDN'T HIT THE BROAD SIDE OF THE BARN WITH HIS SHOT. IT WASN'T LONG BEFORE HE KNEW PRECISELY WHERE THAT SHOT WAS GOING."

– LANNY MCDONALD ON AL MACINNIS

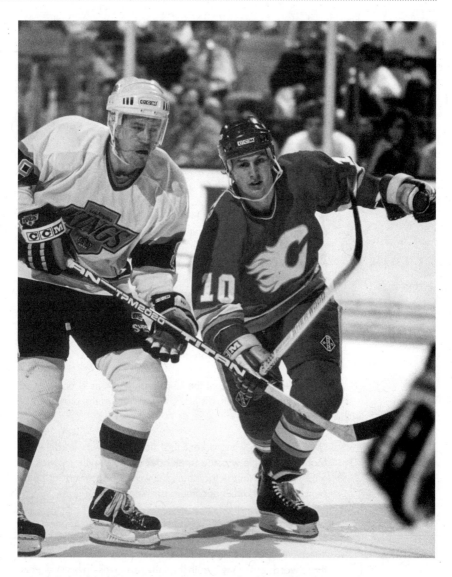

Forward depth and Vernon's opening-round Game 7 heroics aside, the key contributor that spring was MacInnis. Known more for his booming shot than his two-way game, MacInnis led playoff scorers by a six-point margin, with seven goals and 31 points in 22 games. He won the Conn Smythe Trophy as playoff MVP.

Gary Roberts, only 22 at the time, played on the Flames' first line during their 1989 championship season.

"Everyone knows what MacInnis did that spring," McDonald said. "Thirty-plus points is unbelievable for a defenseman. He was that good. That's why he's in the Hall of Fame. When he first came in, he couldn't hit the broad side of the barn with his shot.

It wasn't long before he knew precisely where that shot was going."

In the final, the teams split the first two games in Calgary. Ryan Walter's double overtime goal in Game 3 gave Montreal a 2-1 series lead and had Calgary fans thinking deja vu from the '86 series. The Flames rebounded with 4-2 and 3-2 victories with Game 6 back in Montreal.

McDonald, 36 at the time, was a healthy scratch the previous three games. But coach Crisp knew the future Hall of Famer had a flare for the dramatics and a terrific sense of timing. It was the bottom of the ninth in McDonald's storied career and he had just four goals and 11 points in 40 games of sporadic duty that season. With less than a month remaining in the season, McDonald was at 493 career goals and 999 career points. The milestone of 1,000 points was so close, but 500 goals was seemingly unattainable.

But in a magical three-game run, McDonald scored five goals, then later reached the 500-goal plateau with a marker in his second-last regular season game.

In the deciding game of the Cup final, McDonald broke a 1-1 second-period tie with his first and last goal of the playoffs. The Flames went on to win 4-2.

"McDonald's key ingredient that final year was leadership," Maher said. "He was the ringleader of the bunch. He was the glue that kept things together. He wasn't happy about being benched, but it didn't become a problem, either.

"That last game was a storybook finish for him. When Nieuwendyk had the puck (in that final game), I said on the air, 'there's McDonald open on the right wing.' No sooner were those words out of my mouth than the puck was on his stick, then in the goal. It was fate for him and that team that season."

> "THAT FOURTH LINE COULD BE THE NO.2 LINE ON THE CURRENT TEAM. THERE WAS SO MUCH DEPTH, THEY WERE ABLE TO TRADE A SCORER LIKE BRETT HULL JUST TO GET INSURANCE."
>
> – FLAMES PLAY-BY-PLAY MAN PETER MAHER

No. 15

1948-49 TORONTO MAPLE LEAFS

Turk Broda posted the only shutout of the entire 1948–49 playoffs with a 3–0 win over the Bruins in Game 1 of the semifinals.

THE NHL'S FIRST DYNASTY took place when the Toronto Maple Leafs won six Stanley Cups in 10 years between 1942 and 1951 while employing vastly different lineups.

But despite not being the most proficient regular season team, the most impressive of those six victories was authored by Toronto's 1948-49 squad. And it wasn't just because the Cup win marked the first time any organization had won three consecutive championships.

It was also due to the fact – in spite of The Hockey News making Toronto its pre-season Cup favorite – the '48-49 Cup was the

Leafs' most unlikely NHL championship of that era and the victory stemmed from the squad coming together as a true collective with few, if any, individual standouts.

The team – the NHL's youngest that year at an average age of 24.2 years – entered the season without former captain Syl Apps, who retired after a glorious 10-season career with Toronto. Leafs GM-president Conn Smythe predicted the loss of Apps would be greater than anticipated, but that didn't stop THN from fawning over the lineup:

"Don't be surprised if (new captain Ted 'Teeder') Kennedy, their fighting center, doesn't rise to many an occasion," a THN report advised. "They secured a good journeyman center in (Cal) Gardner, a chap whom the smart Canadiens coach Dick Irvin rates very highly...(the) Leafs still have a young, hard fighting team with players like (Bill) Ezinicki, Kennedy, (Jimmy) Thomson, Max Bentley...the rookies are well-qualified and some of them are future stars...it is a well-handled team and should always be there or thereabouts during the race."

The magazine was right about Kennedy (a career-long Leaf and Hockey Hall of Fame inductee in 1966) stepping up in Apps' stead: through the first 26 games, 'Teeder' led Toronto in scoring.

THE MAPLE LEAFS STARTED THE YEAR WINNING JUST THREE OF THEIR FIRST SIX HOME GAMES AFTER WINNING 22 OF 30 HOME GAMES THE PREVIOUS SEASON.

Unfortunately, the magazine was initially wrong about Kennedy's team; the Maple Leafs started the year winning just three of their first six home games after winning 22 of 30 home games the previous season. After 26 games, Toronto was fifth in the six-team NHL with an 8-12-6 record (in contrast to the league-leading Detroit Red Wings, who were 14-9-2).

The Leafs only had two players over the age of 30 (goaltender and future Hall of Famer Turk Broda, who was 34, and 32-year-old right winger Don Metz) and it showed in their inconsistent play. They could win two games in a row, but just as quickly go on a four-game winless streak.

But if they were a young team, they were also a familiar bunch, having played together or against one another as amateurs in the junior ranks. And it was that familiarity that made the Leafs so close, according to one prominent hockey historian.

"If you look at it on paper, that team is midway through a dynasty, but, in fact, they were an entirely different team than the won that won the Cup in '45, which was entirely different than the one they won in '42," said Kevin Shea, editor of publications and online features for the Hockey Hall of Fame and member of the Society for International Hockey Research. "The Second World War played havoc with the league a great deal and the teams were back to some semblance of normalcy afterward.

"THAT TEAM IS MIDWAY THROUGH A DYNASTY, BUT, IN FACT, THEY WERE AN ENTIRELY DIFFERENT TEAM THAN THE WON THAT WON THE CUP IN '45, WHICH WAS ENTIRELY DIFFERENT THAN THE ONE THEY WON IN '42."
– KEVIN SHEA OF THE HOCKEY HALL OF FAME

"But the 1948-49 team was a good young team and I draw so many parallels between that team and the Edmonton Oilers with Wayne Gretzky and Mark Messier. Both of those teams really grew together.

"Those Maple Leafs knew each other and partied together. (Leafs left winger Harry) Watson and his wife Lil were the patriarch and matriarch of the team, even though they weren't much older than some of the youngest players. The team members all seemed to congregate at their home in East Toronto. So they became close on the ice just as they did off it."

But that sense of closeness never translated into consistent regular season wins that year. So, when by January of 1949, the franchise's malaise hadn't ended – and people were openly worried Toronto wouldn't even qualify for one of the four playoff spots in a six-team league – blame for their troubles was beginning to be assigned.

Certainly some Leafs players were not living up to the hype and hysteria that surrounded them. Center Max Bentley (No. 48 on THN's list of the 100 greatest players in league history) had scored only eight goals two-thirds of the way through the 60-game regular season schedule; a year earlier, he had 26 for the season.

But Leafs coach Clarence 'Hap' Day wasn't about to fault one player in identifying what ailed his charges. That said, by modern-day coaching standards, he was remarkably frank.

"Two years ago, if I asked them to go through a wall, they went through," Day said in February of 1949. "Last year they hesitated questioningly a moment and then went through. This year they tell me to go through first."

"WE'VE BEEN HOT AND COLD ALL SEASON. JUST WHEN WE SEEM TO HIT OUR STRIDE, SOMETHING POPS UP AND WE'RE BACK IN OUR SLUMP AGAIN. THAT'S THE WAY IT HAS BEEN ALL ALONG."

– CAL GARDNER, JANUARY 1949

But the Maple Leafs' salvation that season was their unshakeable faith in one another. Consider this January interview Watson and Gardner gave to The Hockey News:

"If we can ever put any kind of a winning streak together, we will." Gardner said when asked if the team would qualify for the playoffs. "We've been hot and cold all season. Just when we seem to hit our stride, something pops up and we're back in our slump again. That's the way it has been all along."

Added Watson, one of four Hall of Fame players on the Leafs that season: "You hear a lot of talk that our club has suffered a big letdown after winning two successive Stanley Cups, but that's all hogwash...the only thing wrong with us this year is that we are not playing as tight a game as we did last season, and we haven't gotten our share of breaks, either.

"Last season, Lady Luck was constantly smiling at us. Take Max Bentley, for example. He has been scoring relatively few goals this year. He keeps hitting the post, and that's really tough. Another thing that hasn't helped us has been the loss of Syl Apps."

By the end of January, Toronto had a 13-18-10 mark. A moderate improvement in play the rest of the campaign (9-7-3) landed the Maple Leafs the final post-season berth, but only following monumental collapses by the Chicago Black Hawks and New York Rangers – and even then, the Blue and White dropped six of their final nine regular season games heading into the playoffs.

Losing captain Syl
Apps, who led the team
to back-to-back Stanley
Cups the prior two
years, was just one
obstacle the 1948–49
Leafs overcame.

So it was no wonder few people believed the Leafs were in a position to win their Stanley Cup semifinal series against the Boston Bruins, who finished nine points ahead of Toronto in the regular season standings.

But again, Toronto's players believed in themselves.

"They had great confidence they could be Stanley Cup champions, even when the regular season did not unfold in their favor and they didn't play up to expectations," Shea said. "This was not a shy, retiring team in any way, on or off the ice."

Once the playoffs began, the Maple Leafs sprang to life and showed what they were made of.

In their series against the Bruins (whom Toronto had also met in the 1948 playoffs and beaten in five games), the Leafs had a relatively easy go of it. They again beat the Bruins in five games – including a 3-0 shutout by Broda in Game 1, the only shutout posted the entire post-season.

That set up a Cup final date with Detroit, the favorite to dethrone the defending champs, with the Red Wings holding home ice advantage after 12 more regular season wins than Toronto.

None of that made a lick of difference to the Leafs. They swept Detroit in the Cup final for the second straight year – Broda allowed just one goal in each of the final three games – and made the inconsistent regular season irrelevant to their legion of fans.

The Leafs had no representatives on the league's first or second all-star teams and they had just one player in the top 10 in NHL goal-scoring and nobody in the top 10 in assists. The team wasn't about individual accolades, though. It was a true collective effort.

When all the hockey had been played that season, the Leafs had the Cup in their possession once again. And although they joined the '37-38 Hawks as the only Cup-winning teams to finish the regular season with losing records, they'd established a new measuring stick for Cup success – all because of confidence that kicked in just in time.

"They always had that confidence, although they sure scared their fans along the way," said Shea. "They would claim the Cup win wasn't a surprise to them, but it sure was a surprise to people who had watched them all year."

No. 16

2007-08 DETROIT RED WINGS

BABA O'RILEY WAS THE CHOICE OF SONG, but the message from dressing room DJ Chris Chelios was clear: the Detroit Red Wings wouldn't get fooled again.

If the toe-tapping moments before Game 6 of the 2008 Stanley Cup final at Mellon Arena felt a little more angst-ridden than usual for the Wings, it was because of what had happened two nights earlier in Game 5: Detroit had an opportunity to close out Sidney Crosby and the Pittsburgh Penguins with a win on home ice. With the Joe Louis Arena crowd chanting "We want the Cup!" and the champagne corks about to burst, the Motor City was on the verge of complete eruption.

It was party time for the Detroit Red Wings after defeating the Pittsburgh Penguins in Game 6 of the 2008 Cup final.

Then every breathe of air got sucked out of the building when Max Talbot tied the game 3-3 with just 35 ticks left in regulation time.

No Cup; no corks. Just three more periods of hockey before Petr Sykora's power play goal sent the teams back to Pittsburgh, where the Penguins had a stellar 9-1 record during that post-season.

Kris Draper was a veteran center in search of his fourth Stanley Cup with Detroit that spring. Though his team entered the series as favorites and still had two more chances to clinch the championship, he recalls a shift in how people started viewing the matchup.

NO CUP; NO CORKS. JUST THREE MORE PERIODS OF HOCKEY BEFORE PETR SYKORA'S POWER PLAY GOAL SENT THE TEAMS BACK TO PITTSBURGH.

"A lot of people were taking about, now Pittsburgh is the favorite, they're younger, they're faster, they had a great record in their building," he said.

The Wings, of course, had decorated players like Draper and captain Nicklas Lidstrom to lean on, but it was the presence of two guys who didn't even play in the sixth game that went a long way toward calming some nerves.

Chelios and Darren McCarty both took the Game 6 warmup knowing full well they would be scratches for the contest. McCarty remained in full equipment throughout the night, watching the game from the dressing room and dishing out encouragement to teammates between periods.

Chelios, meanwhile, seized the airwaves just before the Wings marched out for the first faceoff. Everybody knew what song was coming because The Who's Baba O'Riley was the anthem of choice before every game that post-season. But Chelios had an extra lyric of motivation for the team before turning things over to the English rockers.

"Chris Chelios, on that last song, just cranked it up and said, 'This is the last time I'm playing this one this year boys,' " Draper relayed. "The little things like that get the guys fired up. Those are the little memories you're going to have that are behind the scenes. Obviously the game is decided on the ice between the

It wasn't just the stars who shone for the Wings in 2007–08; lesser lights like Valtteri Filppula, Brian Rafalski and Mikael Samuelsson all helped the cause.

players, but those are the little things that go a long way in those situations, especially from a Hall of Famer like Chris Chelios and a character guy like Darren McCarty."

As it turned out, Detroit needed every note of inspiration after Marian Hossa scored with less than two minutes to play, slicing the Wings' advantage to 3-2 as visions of Game 5's meltdown no doubt started surfacing in the minds of Hockeytown supporters everywhere.

Sure enough, another golden opportunity came Hossa's way in the dying seconds, but when he couldn't stuff the puck past Red

Wings stopper Chris Osgood, the Cup was finally secured – a fact it took some people a little while to digest.

"Danny Cleary was on the ice and 'Hoss' missed and then the buzzer went, and Cleary, for a good two or three seconds, is just kinda standing there, not realizing that he had just won the Stanley Cup," Draper said. "Finally, 'Ozzie' just dropped his gloves and grabbed him."

"YOU JUST KIND OF HAD THAT FEELING THESE GUYS WERE READY TO TAKE THIS TEAM TO THE NEXT LEVEL."

– KRIS DRAPER

Cleary's temporary disbelief no doubt reflected the feelings of a few Red Wings on a team that had experienced significant turnover since the last the Stanley Cup had visited Michigan in 2002.

In addition to Mike Babcock winning his first ring as a coach, this was the first championship won with Henrik Zetterberg and Pavel Datsyuk (who was a rookie in 2002 and played less than 11 minutes per contest) as Detroit's go-to forwards with longtime captain Steve Yzerman having hung up his skates two years earlier.

Prior to the '08 championship, one of the most popular refrains in the hockey world was that Zetterberg and Datsyuk were great players, but not the kind of guys who can lead you to the Promised Land.

The slick, European-laden Wings had been bounced the previous year in the Western Conference final by the Anaheim Ducks, a team that augmented a skilled core with crushers and bruisers. This led some to believe Detroit was too soft to scale all the way to the mountain top as it had in the pre-lockout era.

Ironically, it was during that six-game loss to Anaheim that Zetterberg and Datsyuk really began proving what they could do in crunch time. The Ducks, playing on home ice, built a 3-0 advantage through two periods in Game 6, leaving them 20 minutes from a trip to the final.

It would have been easy for the game to get away from Detroit at that point, but its two most skilled players simply willed their club back in the mix.

"We made that a hockey game, basically riding 'Pav' and 'Hank,' " Draper said.

Zetterberg scored one goal to make it a 3-1 game, then after Samuel Pahlsson restored Anaheim's three-goal advantage, Datsyuk fired two of his own, nearly bringing Detroit back all the way before falling just one tally shy in a 4-3 loss.

"I remember looking at those guys after the game, they were just physically exhausted with what they did and obviously so disappointed realizing we were that close to tying the game and tying the series and moving it back to Detroit," Draper said. "You just kind of had that feeling these guys were ready to take this team to the next level. That was the one thing I certainly remember in that Anaheim series.

"You could see the fight and the determination in both 'Pav' and 'Hank.' "

And if you didn't catch it that year, there was no missing it in 2008. Zetterberg tied for the playoff lead in both goals (13) and points (27). His third period tally in Game 6 in Pittsburgh turned out to be the Cup winner, as he became just the second European to claim the Conn Smythe Trophy as playoff MVP. Lidstrom was the first when he won the award in 2002 and he added another gold star to his resume in 2008 when he became the first European captain of a Stanley Cup-winning team.

Datsyuk, like Zetterberg, was a two-way force, consistently muting other team's top lines while scoring 10 goals and 23 points in 22 post-season games.

As it turned out, the story arc of Zetterberg and Datsyuk — and the 2008 Wings as a whole — was comparable to the bumpy path taken by Yzerman and Sergei Fedorov a decade earlier, as the Wings looked to end a 40-plus year title drought.

The Yzerman-led Detroit teams lost heart-breaking series to the Toronto Maple Leafs, San Jose Sharks, New Jersey Devils and Colorado Avalanche before finally winning it all in 1997.

The 2008 Wings were preceded by Detroit clubs that had advanced past the second round just once in four playoff seasons despite consistently finishing at or near the top of the league standings.

"When we lost in '06 to Edmonton in the first round, people thought we had too many Europeans," said Detroit GM Ken Holland. "And in 2007 we went to the third round and we needed that playoff experience to help us succeed in 2008. So in that cycle, Zetterberg and Datsyuk are probably Yzerman and Fedorov from years earlier."

The 2008 title wasn't just validation for two superstars; it also did a lot to deconstruct the myth Detroit required a mammoth payroll to strike silver. The Red Wings became the first team to win Cups both before and after the 2004-05 lockout, proving they were just as capable of glory in a salary-cap world as when their fat wallet allowed for a lineup full of stars.

Holland said the organization's approach to building a team didn't really change that much. He believes because the Wings' 2002 championship club had such a high payroll that people often erroneously assume that was also the case with the previous winners in '97 and '98.

"When we won the Cup in 1997 and 98, our payroll was around $30 million," he said. "We spent more money to keep the team together, but we didn't spend any more money than a lot of other teams at the time. And when we won in 2008, we were $5 million below the cap. So three of our four Cups, we were a midmarket team. But people remember the '02 team and because we've had a pretty good run, they lump everything together and say we've always been big spenders."

What was indisputable after 2008 was that the Wings were once again winners, led by two players whose credentials were never questioned again.

"WE SPENT MORE MONEY TO KEEP THE TEAM TOGETHER, BUT WE DIDN'T SPEND ANY MORE MONEY THAN A LOT OF OTHER TEAMS AT THE TIME."

– GM KEN HOLLAND

No. 17

2006-07 ANAHEIM DUCKS

THE GENESIS OF ANAHEIM'S FIRST STANLEY CUP – not to mention the first ever by a West Coast NHL team – actually came the year prior, when a feisty Ducks squad upset Calgary in the first round of the playoffs and went all the way to the conference final where a fellow underdog, the Edmonton Oilers, turfed them in five games.

It was a dream finish for the Niedermayer brothers, Rob and Scott, who got to lift the Stanley Cup together in 2006–07.

One of the principle reasons the Oilers got to that point and beyond was the play of behemoth defenseman Chris Pronger. But with Pronger unhappy in Edmonton that summer, the Ducks followed a popular axiom on the road to further success: If you can't beat 'em, join 'em – or have him join you, as the case was.

And so it came to pass that on July 3, 2006, Pronger was sent to the Ducks in exchange for Joffrey Lupul, Ladislav Smid, two first round draft picks and a second-rounder.

For a Ducks team already featuring future Hall of Famers Scott Niedermayer and Teemu Selanne, plus a fast-maturing kid line of Ryan Getzlaf, Corey Perry and Dustin Penner, Pronger instantly made Anaheim a Stanley Cup favorite. In fact, THN predicted a Ducks Cup that summer.

"I think at the beginning of the season we felt we had the team to go all the way," said star goaltender Jean-Sebastien Giguere. "That was our year to do it. We went to the conference final the year before without expectation and we improved our team that summer by adding Chris Pronger. We felt like if we wanted to work and play together as a team, we could go far."

And they did. Anaheim stormed out of the gates, dropping just two games in regulation in its first 25 contests. Not only did the Ducks have skill, but headlined by the surly, 6-foot-6 Pronger, they were nasty. The team had multiple players not afraid to drop the gloves, including enforcers George Parros and Shawn Thornton, and the hard-nosed Travis Moen. That trio racked up 39 fights during the regular season. To add to the fray, GM Brian Burke picked up an old favorite of his in Brad May, who was acquired in late February for an extra dash of leadership and pugilism.

"We were a heavily penalized team," Getzlaf admitted.

No kidding. In 21 playoff games, the rugged Ducks were shorthanded an incredible 121 times, but thanks to a penalty kill led by defensive wizards Sammy Pahlsson and Rob Niedermayer (who, along with Moen, formed a devastating shutdown line throughout the run), Anaheim managed to stay alive with an 86.8 percent kill rate and even netted two shorthanded goals along the way.

But for all the big names on the roster, Anaheim was not necessarily a team of winners yet and the players did not take that for granted.

"We only had one guy (Scott Niedermayer with the Devils) who had won the Stanley Cup," Getzlaf noted. "Whether you had been in the league for 15 years or two years, we knew winning that Cup may never happen again."

While Andy MacDonald was the top center, playing alongside Selanne and Chris Kunitz, what made the Ducks difficult to defend against was the emerging stars on the second line – Getzlaf, Perry and Penner. All three had been linemates at times in the American League with Portland and came up together to

Anaheim. Despite their youth, the trio combined for 40 points during the run, with Getzlaf (17) and Perry (15) leading the team in scoring. Having veterans such as Pronger, Selanne and Niedermayer around allowed the kids to thrive with some of the pressure deflected.

"I THINK AT THE BEGINNING OF THE SEASON WE FELT WE HAD THE TEAM TO GO ALL THE WAY. THAT WAS OUR YEAR TO DO IT."
– JEAN-SEBASTIEN GIGUERE

"It was an honor to play with some of the guys we did," Getzlaf said. "We wanted to compete for our ice time, we wanted to be on the power play and Mac's line, we wanted to compete with them."

With a formidable top-four defense corps (Pronger, Niedermayer, Beauchemin and Sean O'Donnell), scoring against Anaheim was a tall task. The Ducks surrendered just 2.14 goals per game in the post-season and the fact one of Pronger or Niedermayer could be on the ice virtually the whole game certainly didn't hurt.

"It was great," Giguere said. "Obviously it made my job easier. Those guys were a treat to play with. They're amazing players, so for me, it makes you better if you want to be better – if you want to follow their lead and follow in their footsteps they'll give you the direction. All you have to do is follow them and they'll bring you to the right spot."

And they did. Anaheim steamrolled through the competition, losing just five games total en route to the Cup, including a 4-1 series shellacking of the Ottawa Senators in the final.

"We played hard, no matter what situation we were in," Getzlaf said. "Up in the game, down in the game, it didn't matter – we were a confident group."

Dallas Stars defenseman Stephane Robidas, whose team faced its Pacific Division rivals eight times that year, recalled an Anaheim squad that meant business in every way.

"They played the right way, they had the grit," he said. "They didn't have many holes in their lineup and their 'D' was unbelievable."

Along with the big names such as Pronger, Selanne and Niedermayer, however, the Stars blueliner also gave credit to the lesser-known members of the team for making any contest a tough, 60-minute affair.

> ## "WHETHER YOU HAD BEEN IN THE LEAGUE FOR 15 YEARS OR TWO YEARS, WE KNEW WINNING THAT CUP MAY NEVER HAPPEN AGAIN."
> –RYAN GETZLAF

"People forget a guy like Todd Marchant," Robidas noted, "but he's a guy that brings a lot of speed and kills penalties."

Anaheim was set with two scoring lines – one with finesse, one filled with big, strong youngsters – a shutdown defensive line led by Pahlsson, plus a tough-as-nails fourth line with Marchant in the middle. It was a formidable formula to be sure.

Of course, it all would have gone south had the Ducks not had a very capable backup goaltender in Ilya Bryzgalov.

On April 4, 2007, a family issue arose that threw Giguere's world into turmoil. His wife gave birth to their first child, a baby boy named Maxime Olivier, but doctors were worried about the infant's eyesight. Blindness was a possibility.

The Ducks gave Giguere a leave of absence so he could be with his family during such a crucial juncture, but it also meant he would be missing the final week of the regular season and a portion of the playoffs. Bryzgalov stepped into the No. 1 role and didn't miss a beat.

Bryzgalov held the fort in the first round against Minnesota, ripping off three consecutive victories over the Wild before dropping Game 4 by a score of 4-1. With Giguere back in the mix, the Ducks won Game 5 and earned a matchup with Vancouver in the second round, where they easily dispatched the Canucks in five games.

The Western Conference final provided a little more drama, as the Ducks took on the top seeded Detroit Red Wings, a series many will remember hinging on a controversial Pavel Datsyuk interference penalty late in Game 5. With less than two minutes remaining in a 1-0 game, the Lady Byng winner was hauled off, paving the way for a Scott Niedermayer power play goal.

Selanne scored in overtime to give Anaheim a 2-1 win and 3-2 series lead.

While Ottawa boasted the top three scorers of the playoffs – the line of Daniel Alfredsson, Jason Spezza and Dany Heatley all finished the tourney with 22 points – the Senators got bullied all over the place by the bigger, physical Ducks. In one infamous moment, the usually placid Alfredsson even fired a puck at Scott Niedermayer after a whistle. With nowhere near the depth the Ducks had, the Senators were easy pickings for their Western foe.

In the end, the final was a romp for the Ducks and captain Niedermayer passed the Cup to his brother Rob in a fitting tribute to the team's defensive capabilities both on the back end and up front.

Selanne, Anaheim's elder statesman, finally had his Stanley Cup after 14 seasons in the NHL. The 'Finnish Flash' even had his own entourage of friends and family who made the trip to North America for the run and they did not come away disappointed.

"Obviously we have to wait a long time for something unbeliev-able," Selanne said after the Cup. "And it really makes it even more special. I couldn't of imagined getting the win in our home building. I'm so proud of my teammates. We had one dream together and that's what makes this so special."

"THEY PLAYED THE RIGHT WAY, THEY HAD THE GRIT. THEY DIDN'T HAVE MANY HOLES IN THEIR LINEUP AND THEIR 'D' WAS UNBELIEVABLE."

– DALLAS STARS DEFENSEMAN STEPHANE ROBIDAS

No. 18

1943-44 MONTREAL CANADIENS

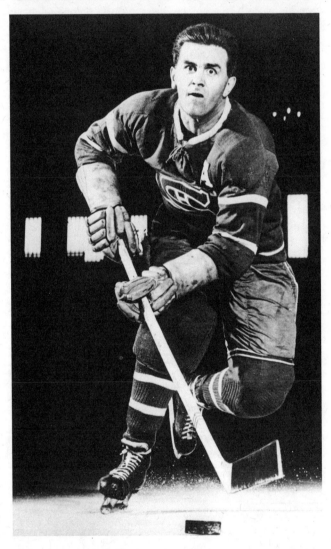

The fire in the eyes of Maurice 'Rocket' Richard of the Montreal Canadiens is an iconic image in the world of hockey.

FOR THE PEOPLE OF QUEBEC, "The Great Darkness" is re-membered as the time when the province was ruled by the iron fist of Premier Maurice Duplessis and his Union Nationale gov-ernment. Duplessis' government, though ripe with corruption and scandal, ruled the province from 1936-39 and 1944-59.

For the hockey fans of Quebec, however, "The Great Darkness" represents the period between 1931 and 1944 when the Montreal Canadiens not only failed to win the Stanley Cup, but almost bumbled their way into oblivion. The Canadiens have long been the standard bearers for excellence in the league, but there was a time 70 years ago when they played to sparse crowds and were whipping boys for the rest of the NHL. In fact, they almost lost the battle for survival to the Montreal Maroons and very nearly were moved to Cleveland.

THE MONTREAL CANADIENS NOT ONLY FAILED TO WIN THE STANLEY CUP, BUT ALMOST BUMBLED THEIR WAY INTO OBLIVION.

That's why the Canadiens team that won the Stanley Cup in 1943-44 is so important to the fabric of the franchise. Had that group not emerged as a hockey powerhouse just as Canada was coming out of the Depression, there's a chance the Canadiens dynasty that followed in the 1950s might never have happened.

A confluence of factors led to the formation of the Habs that season, not the least of which was the emergence of Maurice Richard as a force in the NHL and the fact that Bill Durnan first took his place in the Montreal crease.

But the fact remains that the '43-44 Canadiens were one of the most dominating teams in the history of the game. They did not lose a single game at home that season, going 22-0-3 at the Montreal Forum. Their 38-5-7 overall record gave them a winning percentage of .830, which is second in NHL history only to the 1929-30 Boston Bruins. (Interestingly, if you prorate that campaign over an 80-game schedule, the Canadiens would have had 133 points that season, one more than the 1976-77 Habs, regarded by most as the greatest team ever assembled.)

But much of Montreal's success that season can be attributed to two people most casual hockey fans wouldn't know existed – Tommy Gorman and Len Peto.

Gorman, one of the founding members of the NHL, already had five Stanley Cups with three different teams when he was hired as GM of the Canadiens in 1940. (The only other person in history to win the Stanley Cup with more than one team as GM is Lester Patrick, who won with the Victoria Cougars in 1924-25 and the New York Rangers in 1927-28.) Gorman set about rebuilding the franchise and along with coach Dick Irvin, brought the Canadiens back to contender status.

Peto was an executive and director for Montreal and his role was far less pronounced. But as an executive with Canadair, which supplied the Royal Canadian Air Force with parts and aircraft, Peto was able to negotiate his way around the conscription laws to keep many of the Canadiens players among those with "Home Service Only" status during World War II. While most teams were hit by the war – no team worse than the Boston Bruins, who lost their top line of Milt Schmidt, Woody Dumart and Bobby Bauer to the Canadian Army and Hall of Fame goalie Frank Brimsek to the American effort – the Canadiens were relatively unaffected aside from losing defenseman Kenny Reardon.

"If you look at the team picture, there were only 14 or 15 guys on the team because of the guys being away at the war," said Dick Irvin Jr., a Hall of Fame broadcaster and son of the former Habs coach. "The guys used to practice at night because they were all working during the day."

(Richard and Elmer Lach actually tried to volunteer for the war effort, but were turned down. Richard tried to enlist twice and was turned down both times and while he had his 50-goal season in 1945, both he and the Canadiens flourished even after all the players came back from the war.)

So the Canadiens, with a plethora of talent in a league that was somewhat watered down by the war, went to work. And they did so with Rocket Richard, who had a breakout season with 32 goals and was a scoring force in the playoffs. It was a career that almost never blossomed in Montreal.

The 1943-44 season was just the second in the NHL for Richard and the first had not gone well at all. During his rookie year, Richard suffered a variety of injuries, including a broken leg, and scored just five goals and 11 points in 16 games. Gorman began to wonder whether or not Richard could handle the rigors of playing in the NHL and seriously considered trading his rights.

Irvin pleaded with Gorman not to trade Richard and to give him another chance to live up to his potential. Thankfully, Gorman listened to his coach and Richard rewarded their faith with a breakout season that was a portent of things to come. In the playoffs that year, Richard exploded for 12 goals in just nine games, including a five-goal performance in Game 2 of the first round against the Toronto Maple Leafs.

The next season, Richard scored his history-making 50 goals in 50 games and a superstar was born. Had Richard not had his breakout season and scored 32 goals to help lead the Canadiens to the Cup, who knows how things would have turned out for both him and the organization?

Another significant piece to the puzzle was Durnan, who was a 27-year-old amateur who eschewed the NHL and everything it stood for after a bad experience during a tryout with the Maple Leafs. Durnan had already established himself as a star with the Kirkland Lake Blue Devils and later the Montreal Royals and was fully prepared to play out his career as an amateur before the Canadiens pursued him.

"IF YOU LOOK AT THE TEAM PICTURE, THERE WERE ONLY 14 OR 15 GUYS ON THE TEAM BECAUSE OF THE GUYS BEING AWAY AT THE WAR."
– DICK IRVIN JR., HALL OF FAME BROADCASTER

Durnan held out until 10 minutes before the first game of the season to sign a contract with the Habs, one that embarked him on a Hall of Fame career that included a mind-boggling six Vezina Trophies and six first-team all-star selections in just a seven-season career.

"One of the big keys to that team was Bill Durnan," Irvin Jr. said. "He was ambidextrous and there were times when he would switch his stick from one glove to the other. I remember Max Bentley said one time, 'It doesn't matter what side he's on, you've always got that big glove staring you in the face.' (Former NHL referee) Bill Chadwick maintained Durnan was the best goalie he had ever seen."

For all of his regular season success, though, Durnan won only one more Cup with the Canadiens, in 1945-46. The perception around the NHL was that Durnan was undoubtedly the best goalie in the league in the regular season, but was bettered by Turk Broda of the Maple Leafs in the playoffs.

Despite not dropping a single game at the Forum during the regular season, Montreal lost its first home game of the playoffs that year to Toronto and goaltender Paul Bibeault, who was on loan from the Canadiens. But the Habs dispatched the Leafs in incredibly easy fashion, winning the next four games, including an 11-0 walloping in Game 5.

Montreal won the final in four straight over the Chicago Black Hawks and Richard was no less dominating. In the first Stanley Cup final of his career, Richard scored five goals, including all three tallies in the Canadiens' 3-1 win in Game 2.

In all, the Punch Line of Lach between Toe Blake and Richard accounted for 10 of the Habs' 16 goals in the '44 final. They scored all five goals in the clinching game, including the over-time winner by Blake in a 5-4 victory. In that final overtime game, Durnan stopped Chicago's Virgil Johnson on the first pen-alty shot ever awarded in a Stanley Cup final.

"IN GAME 4, THE CANADIENS WERE DOWN 4-1 AND PEOPLE WERE YELLING 'FAKE!' THINKING THE CANADIENS WERE THROWING THE GAME TO GET ANOTHER GATE."

– DICK IRVIN JR., HALL OF FAME BROADCASTER

"The Canadiens had won the first game in Montreal and the next two in Chicago," Irvin Jr., recalled. "In Game 4, the Canadiens were down 4-1 and people were yelling 'Fake!' thinking the Canadiens were throwing the game to get another gate, but they scored three goals in the third period to send it to overtime be-fore Blake scored."

Despite all the top-end talent Montreal had, they were far from a collection of individual superstars. Only Lach finished in the top 10 in scoring that season and Durnan was the only mem-ber of the Canadiens selected to the first all-star team. Lach, Richard and defenseman Butch Bouchard were named to the second team.

But it did represent the start of something bigger in Montreal. Richard used that season as a springboard to a Hall of Fame career and was a full-blown superstar by the time the Canadiens had made winning the Stanley Cup a habit in the 1950s.

No. 19

1935-36 DETROIT RED WINGS

JACK ADAMS WAS TALKING TO ANOTHER PLAYER on the Detroit Red Wings bench when Pete Kelly jumped over the boards to replace a tired Larry Aurie.

Kelly, a checking-line right winger, wasn't supposed to be on the ice when he took a pass from Herbie Lewis and scored the Stanley Cup-winning goal in a 3-2 victory over the Toronto Maple Leafs in Game 4 of the 1936 final. It was Detroit's first Stanley Cup, but coach-GM 'Jolly' Jack Adams didn't send Kelly onto the ice and he wasn't pleased he went out.

"He still gave him hell when he got back to the bench," said hockey historian Bob Duff.

Adams would loosen up later in the dressing room and have his first taste of alcohol after sipping champagne from the Cup. He won it as a player for the Toronto Arenas in 1917-18, but it was his first as coach and GM. It was also the first of two consecutive Cups for the Red Wings (the last of the NHL's Original Six teams to win it) and the first back-to-back championships by an American team. And the despotic Adams was the team's galvanizing point.

"He was the uniting factor," Duff said. "They all united in hating Jack Adams. They were a real tight bunch. There was a real harmony with the club and they all got along well. That's what carried the day for them – that they genuinely all liked each other and wanted to play hard for each other.

"He was always on them and really never let up. It didn't seem to matter who you were, everybody had a turn in his doghouse."

Adams was the architect of the 1935-36 Detroit Red Wings, but the team was built thanks to owner James Norris Sr., who financed the club from his multi-million-dollar grain empire even as the American economy fell to pieces during the Great Depression. In 1932, Norris bought the franchise that was floundering both on and off the ice and changed its nickname from the Falcons to the Red Wings. When 'Big Jim' took over the team, he became to Adams what Adams was to the players –

demanding. He gave Adams just one year to turn the team around, but unlike previous owners, Norris promised him all the money he needed to do it.

"From the day Norris bought the team he said, 'Tell me what you need to win,' " Duff said. "They'd been rubbing nickels together to try and turn them into quarters up until that point."

The Wings soared to a first-overall tie in 1932-33 and won the American Division the following in season before missing the playoffs in 1934-35. Despite the blip in Adams' plans, he made one of his most important acquisitions late in the season: He traded defenseman Teddy Graham and sent $50,000 cash to the St. Louis Eagles for center Syd Howe and defenseman Ralph 'Scotty' Bowman (no relation to Hall of Fame coach Scotty Bowman).

> ## "FROM THE DAY NORRIS BOUGHT THE TEAM HE SAID, 'TELL ME WHAT YOU NEED TO WIN.' THEY'D BEEN RUBBING NICKELS TO-GETHER TO TRY AND TURN THEM INTO QUARTERS UP UNTIL THAT POINT."
> – HOCKEY HISTORIAN BOB DUFF

"That was probably the moment that put them over the top," Duff said. "They were a good team and then they became a great team when they made that trade."

Howe was the centerpiece of the deal, but the hard-hitting Bowman was an integral part of the trade. He was a big body on the blueline who loved to throw his weight around, especially against his first and favorite target.

"Howie Morenz was the first guy he hit," said Bowman's son, George, "because Howie was the man at the time."

Added Bowman's other son, Gary: "My dad said, 'I hit that SOB and knocked him up into the second row a couple times.' "

Bowman never had more than five points in a season, though in 1934 he became the first player to ever score on a penalty shot. But he solidified a defense corps with Ebbie Goodfellow, captain Doug Young and another bruising blueliner, Wilfred 'Bucko' McDonald, who was runner-up for rookie of the year during the Cup season of '35-36.

"Pete Kelly told me that Bucko McDonald was the hardest hitter he had seen and played with," said Ernie Fitzsimmons, hockey historian and co-founder of the Society for International Hockey Research. "He was a pretty bombastic character.

"Those guys were so important in Jack Adams' system, because he wanted everybody to stay back. You weren't allowed to go up over your own blueline let alone the other one."

Adams was a defense-minded coach during a low-scoring decade and a season when games averaged just 4.33 goals. But despite Adams' approach, the 1935-36 Red Wings finished middle of the pack in goals against (103). They're remembered more for their high-powered offense that scored 124 goals, just two behind the league-leading Maple Leafs.

Detroit actually scored more goals the season prior (127), but the acquisition of center Marty Barry from the Boston Bruins along with Art Giroux for all-star center Ralph 'Cooney' Weiland and Walt Buswell before the start of '35-36 distributed the scoring more evenly. The trade gave Adams two strong scoring lines, allowing him to slide Howe down to the second line and slot Barry between star wingers Aurie and Lewis.

"Adams and Art Ross (Boston's GM) were talking at the 1935 Stanley Cup final," Duff said. "Ross said that if the Bruins had 'Cooney' Weiland it would give them a strong line and Adams said if the Red Wings had Marty Barry they'd win the Cup. They hammered out the deal and Adams turned out to be right.

"They didn't have a No. 1 center until they got him. They had wingers Aurie and Lewis, but really they had been searching for a center to play with those two guys their whole careers."

Barry tied for second in league scoring with 40 points on 21 goals and helped lift Lewis into the top 10 with 37 points. More significantly, the trade gave the Wings an all-around attack. In a low-scoring era with a 48-game schedule, Detroit had four players with 30 or more points, seven with 20 or more and a dozen with 10 or more – tops in all three categories. The team had the second-highest scoring defense as well.

Adams also brought in Kelly from St. Louis and left winger Hec Kilrea from the Maple Leafs to round out the team and help Detroit finish first overall with 24 wins and 56 points. These and other role players bore the Adams trademarks of team toughness and defensive discipline. And although Adams used them sparingly, their lesser lights shined bright in the playoffs. None more legendary than rookie Modere 'Mud' Bruneteau in the early morning of Wednesday, March 25, 1936 at the Montreal Forum.

In the first game of the playoffs, the Wings and Montreal Maroons established a record that has never been broken. The teams went scoreless through regulation, but it wasn't until they went into overtime that the real drama began.

"MY DAD SAID, 'I HIT THAT SOB AND KNOCKED HIM UP INTO THE SECOND ROW A COUPLE TIMES.' "

– GARY BOWMAN, SON OF RED WING RALPH BOWMAN

The teams ended up playing nearly two full games of overtime. Between periods, Detroit staff massaged players with rubbing alcohol and fed them teaspoons of sugar dipped in brandy to keep them going. Wings goalie Normie Smith had stopped 89 shots and Lorne Chabot of the Maroons had made 65 saves when Adams sent out one of his spare parts to end the game.

Bruneteau was the team's extra forward in the playoffs, playing in only 24 regular season games and scoring just two goals. At 2:25 a.m., nearly six hours after the game began, Bruneteau picked up an errant pass from Kilrea and fired a low shot past Chabot at 16:30 of the sixth overtime to end the longest game in league history at 176 minutes and 30 seconds.

Some of the more than 9,000 fans at the Forum who stayed – or left and then returned – to see the end showered Bruneteau with dollar bills. He brought the money into the dressing room and shared it with his teammates. At the same time, McDonald was collecting his own money – $185 from a fan who, before the game, offered him five dollars for every Maroon he knocked down. McDonald iced 37 Maroons that night.

Smith shut out the Maroons again in Game 2, 3-0, and ran his Stanley Cup-record shutout streak to 248 minutes and 32 seconds before Montreal finally scored. He finished the series with a 0.20 goals-against average in a three-game sweep. The Wings went on to defeat the Leafs in four games for their first Stanley Cup. It was a total team effort that even the prickly Adams acknowledged.

"Every player on the team has taken a turn at bringing the house down in these playoffs," Adams said after winning the Cup. "I never saw anything like it."

The victory meant a sweep of every major sports title that season for Detroit, making it the original city of champions with baseball's Tigers winning their first World Series and the Lions taking their first NFL championship in the fall of 1935. The Red Wings went on to become the first American dynasty after three Cup wins and two more appearances in the final during an eight-season span. Barry, Howe and Lewis were all inducted into the Hall of Fame, as was Adams; Norris was inducted as a builder.

Adams remains the only person to have his name engraved on the Stanley Cup as a player, coach and GM.

AT 2:25 A.M., BRUNETEAU PICKED UP AN ERRANT PASS AND FIRED A LOW SHOT PAST CHABOT AT 16:30 OF THE SIXTH OVERTIME TO END THE LONGEST GAME IN LEAGUE HISTORY AT 176 MINUTES AND 30 SECONDS.

No. 20

1999-00 NEW JERSEY DEVILS

Martin Brodeur's 1.61 GAA in the 1999–2000 playoffs was the best among all goalies.

IN THE MIND OF LONG-TIME Devils right winger Randy McKay, the 1999-2000 New Jersey team was more talented than the 1994-95 squad that won the organization's first Stanley Cup. But that doesn't mean the road to their second Cup was easier or less sweet.

"In 95, a lot of things went right for us," said McKay. "In 2000, we had a lot more speed and we had more talent, top-to-bottom.

"When you win your first Cup, guys like (NHL legend) Larry Robinson tell you to appreciate it, because it might not come again. And I did try and appreciate it more the second time. We certainly had a roller-coaster ride in 2000."

The roller coaster wheels began to turn prior to the Devils' first regular season game: the leading scorer from the previous season, Petr Sykora, was under contract yet was embroiled in a mysterious five-day holdout at the start of training camp, while forward Brendan Morrison was a restricted free agent also in holdout mode.

Meanwhile, rumors swirled that John McMullen, the Devils' owner since the team relocated to New Jersey from Colorado in 1982, would be selling the franchise to a conglomerate led by New York Yankees kingpin George Steinbrenner.

At first, none of the off-ice drama seemed to affect the team, which had a 27-10-5-3 record as of mid-January.

"IN 2000, WE HAD A LOT MORE SPEED AND WE HAD MORE TALENT, TOP-TO-BOTTOM."
– RANDY MCKAY

Reliable forwards Sykora and Bobby Holik were smart and steady up front; blueline stalwarts Scott Stevens and Scott Niedermayer played the type of tough, strategically responsible defensive hockey the franchise had become famous for; goalie Martin Brodeur played 34 of the team's first 37 games, racked up wins and played in the All-Star Game; and GM Lou Lamoriello repatriated crafty veteran Claude Lemieux in November by acquiring him from Colorado for Brian Rolston and a first round draft pick.

As well, the Devils were getting important contributions from some of their young players. In particular, Scott Gomez (their first round pick in the 1998 draft) and defenseman Brian Rafalski (who had played the previous season with HIFK Helsinki of the Finnish League) were emerging as key components in New Jersey's success.

However, the seeds were being planted for a late-season mutiny that ended with the Devils firing coach Robbie Ftorek a handful of days before the playoffs began.

Ftorek – a former NHLer who had coached the Devils' American League affiliate in Albany, N.Y. to a Calder Cup championship in 1994-95 – was never regarded as the most laid-back personality in the game.

But the pressures of coaching the Devils were not sitting easily on Ftorek's shoulders – and it showed in the pattern of alienation he established with many people involved in the game.

Ftorek drew the ire of Ken Daneyko when he sat out the longtime Devils blueliner for what would have been his 999th career NHL game, causing him to miss playing his 1000th game at home in front of family and friends.

When Ftorek made Lyle Odelein a healthy scratch in November, the defender was clearly unimpressed and made it known in the media.

Ftorek embarrassed Rafalski in December when the Devils traveled to Chicago and Rafalski was scratched the night his family came to see him play in the NHL for the first time.

When Devils assistant coaches Larry Robinson, Slava Fetisov and Jacques Caron were late for the team bus after a workout in San Jose, Ftorek refused to hold the ride for them and left the trio at the arena.

Ftorek was also fined $10,000 by the league and served a one-game suspension for throwing a bench onto the ice in Detroit at the end of January.

"THAT WAS THE FIRST TIME IN THE HISTORY OF THE CONFERENCE FINALS THAT A TEAM CAME BACK TO WIN FROM 3-1 IN A SERIES...WE WOKE UP AFTER GAME 4 AND WE PULLED IT OFF."

– CLAUDE LEMIEUX

In defense of his coach, Lamoriello attempted to change the chemistry of the team and weed out as many unhappy Devils as he could: Odelein was traded to Phoenix for Deron Quint and a third round pick; defenseman Sheldon Souray was shipped to Montreal for blueliner Vladimir Malakhov; and Morrison and center Denis Pederson (upset about a lack of playing time) were traded to Vancouver in a blockbuster deal for Alexander Mogilny.

"We traded two players who we may have had to expose (in the NHL's then-looming expansion draft) for one talented veteran who will play on our top two lines," Lamoriello said of the Mogilny deal at the time. "I think that's in keeping with our organization's philosophy. We believe in team composition of one-third veterans, one-third mid-age and one-third young players; and even after picking up Claude Lemieux, Malakhov and Mogilny, that's what we have."

Around the same period, McMullen conditionally sold the team to the Steinbrenner-led conglomerate for $175 million. It was a decision he would publicly regret later that year when the Devils went on their championship run – but the die had been cast.

The same appeared to be true for Ftorek's fate with the organization. Although Odelein was in Arizona and out of the picture, his words from March of 2000 proved prophetic.

"I'll just say the team isn't as happy as everyone lets on," Odelein said at the time. "Robbie took the wind out of my sails. He's the first coach I didn't get along with. A lot of other players have trouble with him.

"This Devils team is so talented. They'll pull together as a group. Guys like Randy McKay and Marty Brodeur will take charge."

Eventually, that was indeed the case. Unfortunately for Ftorek, the Devils lost 10 of 16 games beginning in mid-February – and on March 23, with just eight regular-season games remaining, Lamoriello fired his coach and replaced him with Robinson.

"It's a decision that did not come overnight," Lamoriello said at the time. "It's one that's been mounting up…I don't think putting Larry Robinson in charge is too late. I think waiting longer would have been too late."

Looking back at this move nearly a decade later, Lemieux feels some sympathy for Ftorek.

"I thought Robbie did a great job," Lemieux said. "He was a good coach and he loved what he did and helped the team tremendously. The only thing I noticed when I got there was that he didn't seem like he was on the same page as the rest of the coaching staff.

"That's probably what led to his firing. Even though we were in first place in the league, that's what might've been behind it, because I felt it was everybody else against him, or him against everybody else."

"Robbie had a strict set of rules – and those rules applied to every guy on the team," added McKay. "I got along okay with him, but it was a shock when he was let go."

That said, it was clear the decision to remove Ftorek was appropriate.

"The players weren't responding to him," Daneyko said in March of 2000. "At times you have to be adjustable and willing to change. I don't know if Robbie was willing to change. He wasn't getting the most out of us."

Added Robinson: "(Ftorek is) such a strong-willed person, he kept a lot inside of him. I could tell there was a lot of pressure on him. Deep down he was carrying a lot inside of him. I don't think any job is worth your health."

Robinson, a legend in his days as a Montreal Canadiens defenseman, couldn't turn the Devils' fortunes around during the remainder of the regular season (New Jersey went 4-4 in its final eight games). But his player-friendly approach was like manna from heaven to a team worn down by Ftorek.

"Claude Lemieux told us there's not a better man in hockey than Larry Robinson," Holik said after the Devils won the Cup that year. "Scott Stevens told us he'd been around a long time and that we're not ever going to do better than Larry, or for that matter, Slava and Jacques. He said, 'Let's play for them, let's do it.' "

The results of the relaxed-yet-focused Devils team were immediately on display in the post-season: New Jersey swept Florida in the first round, then dispatched the Toronto Maple Leafs in a six-game, second-round victory.

Once they got to the conference final, the Devils met a hungry Philadelphia Flyers team and wound up trailing the series 3-1. That's when Robinson's angry side revealed itself. He went on a rant that would come to be known as "The Tirade" after Game 4 – and the players heard it loud and clear.

"That series was the toughest," Lemieux said. "That was the first time in the history of the conference finals that a team came back to win from 3-1 in a series. We were just shocked to be in that position in that series. We woke up after Game 4 and we pulled it off."

In the Cup final, New Jersey took on the defending champion Dallas Stars. The Devils stomped all over their opponents in Game 1 (winning 7-3), but the Stars fought back and their triple overtime, 1-0 win in Game 5 extended the series to a sixth game in Dallas.

Game 6 was another overtime thriller – but this time, the Devils got the game-and-series-winner when 25-year-old center Jason Arnott scored at 8:20 of double-overtime to give New Jersey the Cup.

In the on-ice celebrations after the game, Robinson wore the jersey of Elias, who was in the hospital after being knocked out by Derian Hatcher in the first period. It was a subtle yet typical act by the anti-Ftorek – and it did not go unappreciated.

"What's good about (Robinson)?" Holik said after the Cup win. "What isn't? He's honest. It's hard to find a man in hockey like that, but that's why we love to play hard for him."

Robinson was humble in victory.

"I wish I could describe it," Robinson said when asked what he felt like when Arnott scored. "But it is an unbelievable feeling. I mean, I have had these feelings as a player and I have had them as an assistant, but what we have gone through since I took over has just been a fairy tale for me."

To Lemieux, the Devils' 1999-00 team was as balanced as it was talented.

"We had great leadership, but you also need those young guys, players coming out of nowhere and surprising everybody," Lemieux said. "There always seems to be one of those every year on teams that win.

"There was a lot of expectations on guys like (2000 Conn Smythe Trophy winner) Scotty Stevens, Brodeur and myself, but the Maddens and Gomezes, and guys like Mogilny who chipped in at the right time late in the year and in the playoffs were valuable, too.

"It was just a very talented team."

"I WISH I COULD DESCRIBE IT. BUT IT IS AN UNBELIEVABLE FEELING."
– COACH LARRY ROBINSON

No. 21

1993-94 NEW YORK RANGERS

Mark Messier, often credited as the greatest leader the game has ever seen, captained the Rangers to their first Stanley Cup win in 54 years in 1994.

THERE ARE FEW PLACES IN THE WORLD that know how to party like New York City. And in 1994, the Big Apple celebrated the New York Rangers' first Stanley Cup since 1940 with the biggest party the NHL has ever seen.

It began in Brighton Beach, where the team's group of Russians organized a wild private team party. And when the celebration went public, all of New York got involved.

"Three generations of Rangers fans had not seen a championship," said TV analyst Glenn Healy, the 1993-94 team's backup netminder. "You can imagine the thirst for them to celebrate the championship…from the parade to Radio City Music Hall, it was an incredible ride with incredible emotion."

The Cup was seen being walked down Broadway Ave., on The Late Show with David Letterman and in police helicopters over Manhattan. Motorcades of New Yorkers followed the Cup to parties after it had been noticed riding shotgun in someone's car.

The trophy went through so much in '94 that the rules surrounding its stewardship were changed and the Hall of Fame's 'Keepers of the Cup' were created. No longer were players simply handed Stanley and told to go on their merry way, the Cup now had 24/7-chaperones who guarded it like a newborn baby.

"It totally changed from that moment on," Healy said.

But the party was never a sure thing. The Rangers had won the Presidents' Trophy that year, but had done the same two seasons prior where they were unceremoniously bounced in the second round of the playoffs. A Cup was no sure thing.

New coach 'Iron' Mike Keenan was known for being hard on his players and questions surrounding Keenan's treatment of the players began as early as four games into the pre-season when he scheduled two-a-day scrimmages. The perceived poor treatment continued during the early part of the regular season, when Keenan benched pretty much everyone at one time or another.

"They have to learn the difference between being an average performer and being a top performer," said an unapologetic Keenan at the time.

Trips to the doghouse weren't sole domain of role players, either. Hall of Fame defenseman Brian Leetch felt Keenan's wrath, as did the longest-tenured Ranger, James Patrick; so did good-guy Ed Olczyk and uber-talented sophomore blueliner Sergei Zubov, who went on to lead the team in scoring (the first defenseman to do so for a first-overall team).

"I guess that's a possibility," Keenan said when asked if his tactics were creating scared, uptight players. "But it's better to find out who can handle these situations in October than in the springtime."

The Rangers began with a 4-5-0 start and Keenan was quoted as saying it'd take until Christmas before the players got used to his system – and presumably him as well. But it didn't take that long. By Nov. 14 the Blueshirts were 12-5-2, in first place, atop the league in power play and penalty-killing percentage and already had nine shorthanded goals.

"One of the things Mike did so well as a coach," reflected Adam Graves, who that season Keenan called the best left winger he had ever coached, "we won a lot of games in the first period that year because you knew you had to be ready to play from the drop of the puck, otherwise you weren't going to play.

"He had a way of galvanizing the guys."

GM Neil Smith also did his part. One of Keenan's main complaints early in the season was that the Rangers simply weren't tough enough and too easily pushed around by bigger, grittier teams.

Looking back at it now, Graves doesn't necessarily agree.

"We had a real presence and we were a big team back in those days," he said. "Jeff Beukeboom, Jay Wells, Joey Kocur to name a few…and then our best player up front, Messier, being probably one of our toughest guys."

Nevertheless, Keenan felt the trading of Tie Domi and Kris King to Winnipeg the season before had left a huge hole, so Smith moved Patrick and Darren Turcotte to Hartford for gritty iron-man Steve Larmer and noted pugilist Nick Kypreos. With Beukeboom, Kypreos and Larmer – whom Keenan had loved when he coached in Chicago – in the lineup, the Rangers were set to play a more Keenan-esque game.

New York went on a 14-game unbeaten streak (12-0-2) and matched the franchise's best point total after 30 games with a 21-6-3 mark. By mid-December, goaltender Mike Richter had set a team record with a 20-game personal unbeaten streak. At the end of the season, he had posted a team record 42 wins.

When the all-star break arrived, New York was firmly atop the league standings with 63 points and Keenan, for once, had little to gripe about.

"The best winning percentage, first in penalty-killing, very close to the top in power play, most shorthanded goals, best GAA; you'd have to give them an 'A' based on those categories," the coach said at the time. "And I'm a tough marker."

After the all-star break the Rangers continued rolling, going 7-1-1, led by captain Mark Messier's 18 points. But as the trade deadline approached, Keenan and GM Smith recognized that, as good as the team was, it wasn't perfect. The Rangers were largely a veteran squad with 12 players aged 29 to 34 and

Keenan had basically used three lines and four defensemen for much of the season. Smith, who had made 47 trades in his four-plus seasons as GM of the Rangers, went to work.

"KEENAN IS PROBABLY THE BEST COACH I'VE PLAYED UNDER. HE HAS A GREAT ABILITY TO READ A GAME FROM A LOT OF DIFFERENT PERSPECTIVES."

– MARK MESSIER

New York acquired four players at the trade deadline. Craig MacTavish and Glenn Anderson were brought in, bringing the number of Cup-winning ex-Oilers to seven – MacTavish, Anderson, Messier, Graves, Beukeboom, Kevin Lowe and Esa Tikkanen. As well, Stephane Matteau and Brian Noonan, another pair of former Keenan players, were acquired from Chicago. Among those on their way out, high-scoring speedsters Mike Gartner and Tony Amonte.

"For us, it was one of those things where we were in first place and people would have said 'Wow,' " Graves remembered. "But as it turned out, with the grind and everything else, it proved to be the winning formula. You have to give a ton of credit to Neil Smith, he did a fantastic job in so many ways...great mix of youth and older veterans."

Added Smith after the season: "Larmer made us a great team for the regular season. The other moves made us a great playoff team."

A shift from the wing to center motivated the mercurial Alex Kovalev and gave the Rangers the balanced attack they'd been looking for all season. Playing on a line with Larmer, the 21-year-old Kovalev went on a tear, scoring eight goals and 20 points in nine games.

"He played a vital role for us," Graves said. "He grew so much throughout the whole season."

With Messier centering the top line flanked by 52-goal man Graves and Leetch and Zubov patrolling the blueline, the Rangers had one of the league's deepest, most feared attacks heading into the post-season.

In Round 1 they rolled over their suburban New York cousins, the Islanders, with a four-game sweep. Leetch and Richter led the way. The high-scoring defenseman tallied eight points in the series. Richter had two shutouts, in Games 1 and 2, and allowed just three goals in total. The clean-sheets were the first consecutive shutouts to start a Rangers post-season series since 1940, the year of their last Cup.

"Was it 1940?" Richter winced when reminded at the time of the foreboding date. "Perfect."

"IT WAS ALMOST SURREAL, THE WHOLE CELEBRATION. WINNING IN NEW YORK AFTER 54 YEARS, IT'D BE TOUGH TO EXPERIENCE A GREATER FEELING."

– ADAM GRAVES

With a 4-1 series win over Washington in the second round, the Rangers ran their record to 16-3-2 since the trade deadline; everything was great on Broadway, even between coach and players.

"Keenan is probably the best coach I've played under," Messier said during the Washington series. "He has a great ability to read a game from a lot of different perspectives."

But that's where the smooth sailing ended.

The Rangers went up against the New Jersey Devils in the Eastern Conference final. New York lost Game 1 in double-overtime before winning the next two contests with a 4-0 Game 2 shutout and a double-overtime Game 3 victory on a Matteau winner.

New York then lost Games 4 and 5 and was facing elimination when captain Messier stood up and guaranteed a win, vowing, "We will be back for Game 7." Down 2-0 late in the second period of Game 6, Messier set up a goal by Kovalev to get the Rangers on the board. He then had one of the best third periods in hockey history.

The Hall of Famer scored the tying, winning and insurance goals in the final stanza, cementing his reputation as one of the best leaders who ever strapped on the blades.

"He's the greatest clutch player in the game," said New Jersey Devil Bernie Nicholls after the game. "When the chips are down, I want Messier."

Keenan added after the game: "That has to be one of the most impressive performances by a hockey player in the history of this league."

If Game 6 was exciting, Game 7 at Madison Square Garden was heart-stopping. For the third time in the series, the game went to double-overtime after New Jersey's Valeri Zelepukin scored with eight seconds to play to tie the game 1-1. For the second time, it was Matteau who played the hero, scoring to send the Rangers to the Cup final and a date with destiny.

If Matteau was the hero and Messier the titan against New Jersey, Leetch was Mr. Steady. He entered the final tied for third in scoring, second in assists, first in defenseman scoring, third in power play points, first in game-winners and first in plus-minus. He had been on the ice for 44 of his team's 60 post-season goals.

New York faced the Vancouver Canucks for the Stanley Cup. The teams had been separated by 27 points in the standings that season, but the dynamic Pavel Bure had been on a tear with Vancouver and was backed-up offensively by Trevor Linden. In goal, the Canucks had a similarly-hot Kirk McLean.

In what is considered one of the best finals of the modern era, just two goals separated the squads during the seven-game series. When it was all said and done, Leetch had won the post-season scoring title and MVP honors.

"You'd be hard-pressed to find a guy who put on a better show winning the Conn Smythe Trophy than Brian did controlling the games in all three zones," Graves said.

Messier had become the first player to captain two different teams to the Cup and the Russian Rangers – Kovalev, Zubov, Alexander Karpovtsev and their leader on and off the ice, Sergei Nemchinov – became the first Russian-trained players to win hockey's Holy Grail.

After 54 years, the pressure was finally off – and the party was on.

"It was almost surreal, the whole celebration," Graves recalled. "Winning in New York after 54 years, it'd be tough to experience a greater feeling."

No. 22

2008-09 PITTSBURGH PENGUINS

The city of Pittsburgh came out to celebrate Marc-Andre Fleury, Sidney Crosby and the rest of the Penguins after they defeated the Red Wings in the 2009 final.

THEIR STRUGGLE was, in the end, their salvation.

The starting point for the third Stanley Cup title won by the Pittsburgh Penguins was July 2, 2008 – the day winger Marian Hossa declared he had signed with the Detroit Red Wings because they provided him "the best chance to win a Cup."

That decision, and those words, changed everything.

The Penguins had acquired Hossa in March 2008 to solidify their chances at returning to the final for the first time since winning back-to-back titles in 1992 and '93. He was with the Penguins to play on a line centered by playmaking star Sidney Crosby, who in three previous NHL seasons had not benefited from a star sniper to his right or left.

Crosby and Hossa excelled in the 2008 playoffs. Crosby finished tied for the points lead, while Hossa was third in goals, and even though the Penguins lost a hard-fought six-game final to the veteran Detroit Red Wings there was a belief among players Hossa would re-sign as a free agent and help finish the job in 2009.

"It's a personal decision," defenseman Brooks Orpik said. "But I don't think you can say (management) didn't do everything to keep him."

Three offers were made to Hossa by GM Ray Shero; five-, six-, and seven-year deals at more $7 million per season. Hossa declined each one before Shero opted to move on. He had already traded away a top-six left wing in Ryan Malone, who was the first Pittsburgh-born player in Penguins history, and there was work to do to keep his nucleus together.

That work wrapped over a frenzied few days in July, when Shero inked long-term deals with Orpik, center Evgeni Malkin and goalie Marc-Andre Fleury. Those three would join Crosby and center Jordan Staal as the Penguins' core, one Shero believed could contend for the Cup on a year-to-year basis.

"I've always said I'm interested in guys that want to be here," Shero said. "Players like Brooks, Geno and Marc-Andre want to play for the Pittsburgh Penguins. Those are the guys I want to keep."

Still, the pursuit of Hossa, and his perceived cold-blooded departure, left a bitter taste that could only be washed away by one tonic.

"I don't think you can find anybody in this room that didn't want it," Staal said of a final rematch with the Red Wings, who had lifted the Cup at Mellon Arena while Penguins players watched.

"It wasn't just 'Hoss,' because that was his decision. It was us wanting to beat the guys that beat us. We always looked at it like they took our title."

However, the journey to a second showdown with the Red Wings was one befitting the previous Penguins' title teams – clubs that battled adversity in the regular season and tumultuous off-seasons and were better for it during the playoffs.

Entering his third full season as coach, Michel Therrien was armed with a new three-year contract and a battle-tested group with unrivaled upside. A strict disciplinarian, Therrien oozed confidence in training camp, which was cut short because of the Penguins' trip to Sweden for the NHL Premiere series.

By the time they arrived in Stockholm, ominous signs were abound. Top defenseman Sergei Gonchar was set to miss five months because of surgery to repair a separated shoulder, sustained in the first pre-season game. That injury forced prospect Alex Goligoski into the lineup before he was ready and it left the power play in the unwanted spot of Malkin playing the right point – a role he had said during the 2008 final he didn't prefer because of his discomfort with the defensive responsibilities.

Also, free-agent acquisition Miroslav Satan, a right winger, appeared early to be a style mismatch with Crosby, who spent much of the early months fielding questions about Hossa's departure.

"EVERYBODY SEEMS TO HAVE FORGOTTEN WHAT WE WENT THROUGH TO GET TO THE PLAYOFFS."

– BROOKS ORPIK

Still, the Penguins started well enough and appeared to be in a groove by November after a swap with Dallas of defenseman Darryl Sydor for Philippe Boucher.

Fleury was lost for a month in mid-November because of a groin injury and two weeks into that stretch Penguins went into a funk.

Actually it was a freefall, one that anguished Crosby, who couldn't find his regular level of big-time production.

Gonchar returned in February, but the Penguins were blown out at Toronto. That left the Penguins 10th in the East and five points from a playoff spot with 25 games remaining.

"You tried to stay positive," left winger Matt Cooke said. "But realistically you realized there wasn't a lot of time to turn this thing around."

Shero was not with the club for that Toronto game because of family matters that needed attention in Pittsburgh. He awoke the morning of Feb. 15 and flew to Uniondale, N.Y., where the Penguins played the Islanders the next day.

Upon arriving at the team hotel he summoned Therrien to his room. The conversation was short.

"He said, 'We're making a change,' and I didn't need to hear anything else," Therrien said after his firing.

Shero turned to Dan Bylsma, a former NHL player and the first-year coach of the Penguins' American League affiliate Wilkes-Barre/Scranton. It was Byslma's first year as a head coach at any level.

He entered a dire situation speaking positively, but one with a captain who was at his career-low point.

"It was the worst," Crosby said. "I knew something was wrong and I didn't know how to fix it."

Two weeks after Bylsma was hired, Shero shipped popular defenseman Ryan Whitney to Anaheim for left wing Chris Kunitz and a prospect. Kunitz was targeted to play with Crosby, but Shero wanted more for his franchise's face.

He found more in the form of veteran right winger Bill Guerin, who was acquired at the deadline from the New York Islanders. Shero also picked up winger Craig Adams, a former Cup-winner with Carolina, off waivers. To make room for both players he made the tough call of assigning Satan, who had scored 17 goals, to the AHL for cap-space relief.

Upon joining the Penguins in Florida, Guerin busted on Crosby as his first act.

"That set a tone right away," forward Max Talbot said. "He comes in and beaks our captain in front of everybody. It was like, 'Let's go have some fun, fellas.' "

The Penguins closed on an 18-3-4 run, jumping from 10th on the day Bylsma was hired to fourth at the finish and home-ice advantage in the first round of the playoffs.

"It's funny, but everybody seems to have forgotten what we went through to get to the playoffs," Orpik said in the summer of 2009. "I'm not saying once we got to the playoffs it was easy, because it wasn't.

"But we had worked so hard to get to the playoffs that I don't think anybody was ever rattled by what we had to go through in the playoffs. I'd say that going back to losing in the (2008) final and all those guys (six forwards) that summer, watching 'Gonch' go down and seeing a coaching change – well, that all prepared us for the playoffs.

"The hard part was over."

Not quite. The Penguins did get tested physically by the Flyers in a six-game Round 1 series. They also rallied to win four of five after dropping Games 1 and 2 at Washington in Round 2, including a Game 7 victory that featured Fleury's highlight-feel denial of Capitals star Alex Ovechkin on a breakaway.

The Hurricanes were easy pickings for the Penguins in the Eastern final and after a sweep Crosby, Gonchar and Malkin – the captain and his alternates – touched the Prince of Wales Trophy as a sign of their intentions for the next round.

"We didn't touch it last year and look what happened," Gonchar said. "Better luck is what we (were) thinking."

The thinking around the hockey world when the Penguins lost Games 1 and 2 at Detroit was probably, "Here they go again." Pittsburgh was again down, 2-0, with the final returning to Mellon Arena.

However, they took Games 3 and 4, the latter of which featured Staal's series-changing shorthanded goal. A 5-0 blowout loss at Detroit in Game 5 left everybody but the Penguins stunned.

"Many people thought they won the series that night," Bylsma said. "We knew they hadn't won anything but a third game."

Staal and Fleury starred in a Game 6 victory, and Talbot's two goals in Game 7 combined with a last-second save by Fleury on defenseman Nicklas Lidstrom completed the improbable comeback.

Hossa finished the series without a goal. Crosby led all goal-scorers with 15 and Malkin was the Conn Smythe winner with 36 points – the most by a player since 1993.

"I wanted to prove that he was wrong," Talbot said of Hossa. "We were his best chance to win the Cup."

No. 23

1960-61 CHICAGO BLACKHAWKS

Stan Mikita had his name engraved once on the Stanley Cup, with the Blackhawks in 1960–61, but many feel he and the team should have won more.

THE ONLY TEAM EVER to win five consecutive Stanley Cups should have, by all rights, made it six in a row. Except for Chicago's Kids 'n' the Hall.

The Montreal Canadiens dynasty of the late 1950s should have carried through into the early 1960s as well because most of their marquee players and future Hall of Famers were in their prime. Jean Beliveau, Boom Boom Geoffrion and Dickie Moore – three of the top 42 stars in the history of the game according to The Hockey News' authoritative book from 1997, The Top 100 NHL Players of All-Time – were all 29 when that 1960-61 season started. Defenseman Doug Harvey was 35. Henri Richard was 24, goalie Jacques Plante was 31 – three more names also among the top 30 players of all-time.

The opening round playoff series between the Canadiens and the young Black Hawks had the makings of a David vs. Goliath battle. The Habs were 22 games above .500 that season and accumulated 92 points, the eighth most in the history of the game at that time. The Hawks were just five games above .500, but 1960-61 marked the dishevelled franchise's first winning season, shockingly, in 15 years.

Chicago's greenhorns included 22-year-old Bobby Hull and 20-year-old Stan Mikita. Those two, along with 24-year-olds Bill Hay and Murray Balfour were the top-scoring Black Hawks. Good thing the Hawks had 29-year-old Glenn Hall between the pipes and a veteran defense that included Pierre Pilote, who was on the verge of winning three straight Norris Trophies.

"We had Glenn Hall in goal," is how Hull summed up Chicago's 1961 Stanley Cup victory 49 years later. "If he's not the greatest to ever play goal, then he's one of the greatest. We had defensemen by the likes of Dollard St-Laurent, who had won four Cups with Montreal, and tough, defensive guys like Al Arbour, who had been with Detroit, Jack Evans, who was a stalwart with the Rangers, and Pierre Pilote and Elmer Vasko. When you look at those defense pairings and goaltending, this was why we won it."

"IF HE'S NOT THE GREATEST TO EVER PLAY GOAL, THEN HE'S ONE OF THE GREATEST."
– BOBBY HULL ON GOALIE GLENN HALL

According to Hall, the Hawks entered that semifinal series against the five-time defending champions "with nothing to lose. We were the only ones who thought we had a chance."

After getting blitzed 6-2 in the opening game in Montreal, Chicago bounced back for a 4-3 win in Game 2 when Eddie Litzenberger broke a tie with less than three minutes remaining. Game 3 in Chicago turned out to be the pivotal one. When Balfour scored 12:12 into the third overtime period, it was like the bells going off to end Rocky Balboa's comeback round against Apollo Creed – game on.

"I couldn't believe how ready they were to be knocked off," Mikita recalled. "We went into the series with gumption, but it wasn't until that triple overtime game that it registered with us. This could be really big. We have a helluva chance to beat these guys."

Mikita remembers the goal as though it happened yesterday. He was playing the left point on the power play and partially whiffed on a blast. The off-speed shot handcuffed a defender and the puck went in front of the net to Balfour, who put it past Plante.

"It was one o'clock in the morning in Chicago," Mikita said. "The place went nuts. I have never heard that stadium go through what happened that night. The fans stayed in their seats and applauded until we came back out. That was unheard of in those days."

Chicago hadn't won a Stanley Cup since 1938, a 23-year drought, the longest in NHL history at the time.

The Canadiens rallied like champions in Game 4, outshooting the hometown Hawks 60-21 in a 5-2 humbling.

"What happened next you could never make up," Hull remembered. "The Canadiens were a team that never got shut out, going something like (88) straight games scoring at least a goal. Well, Glenn Hall shuts them out 3-0 in Montreal, then wins the series in Chicago with another 3-0 win. That's all you need to know to tell how good he was."

In what now seems anticlimactic, Chicago beat the fourth-place Red Wings 4-2 to win the 1961 Cup, the decisive game being a 5-1 Hawks victory in Detroit April 16.

"We tried to get back to Chicago that night, but there was a freak snowstorm in Detroit," Hull said. "I was so darned young, there was excitement and plenty of it. I got drinking beer on the bus back to the hotel and I took Mike Wirtz' dirty old felt hat and got sick as a dog. I wasn't up for any more of the festivities in Detroit. That kind of put the damper on going back to Chicago and having a swarm of people waiting for us at the airport."

As is the case with many Cup champions, they all figured they'll be back to win it again. But for Hull, Mikita and Hall, three legends of the game all among the top 17 all-time players according to THN's list, that was their first and only Cup in 57 combined years of service.

The one thing all three men agree on is that the '60-61 Hawks may be the most decorated Chicago team, but it wasn't the most talented.

"We had better teams later, but I don't know if we had a more dedicated team playing for each other," Hall said. "We had a good, solid team. The defense was excellent. They took away rebounds. Pierre and 'Moose' (Vasko), Al, Jack, Dolly, they weren't interested in scoring goals – well, Pierre may have been. But boy, oh boy, the others were so defensive. If you're going to win, you have to play defense. It was a good team to be a goalkeeper behind them."

Said Mikita: "I'm not sure if that team was any better than some of the other teams that both Bobby and I played on, but it had more confidence."

The offense was led by the 'Million Dollar Line' with Hull, Balfour and Hay. It was Balfour's best season by far, Hay led the team in scoring and Hull was just getting into a groove as a premier goal-scorer. He followed up 1960-61 with his first of five 50-goal seasons.

> ## "THE PLACE WENT NUTS. I HAVE NEVER HEARD THAT STADIUM GO THROUGH WHAT HAPPENED THAT NIGHT. THE FANS STAYED IN THEIR SEATS AND APPLAUDED UNTIL WE CAME BACK OUT. THAT WAS UNHEARD OF IN THOSE DAYS."
> – STAN MIKITA

Mikita and Ken Wharram played with Doug Mohns on the 'Scooter Line' in the mid-1960s, but in that championship season, Ab McDonald was the left winger.

"Then we had some seasoned players on a third line and for penalty-killing," Hull said. "Eric Nesterenko, Eddie Litzenberger, Tod Sloan, Ron Murphy; and big Earl Balfour could skate all night. When you look at it, we had a group of guys who fit the bill to win."

Added Hall: "Nobody mentions Nesterenko too much, but he was head and shoulders above anybody defensively (among the forwards). He and Bill Hay were absolutely great defensively. We were just starting to get really good offensively. Murray Balfour had a great, great series. He played so well. He was always knocked down on the ice when he scored because he'd get into that zone that the defensive team never wanted you to be in."

The Conn Smythe Trophy for playoff MVP wasn't created until 1965, but had they given it out in 1961, Pilote probably would have been the winner. He led the Hawks with three goals and 15 points in 12 post-season games, a sharp increase from his six goals and 35 points in 70 regular season games in which he was eighth in team scoring.

"Pierre was a good defenseman for a number of years, but in that playoffs he was exceptional," Hull said. "He was always heads-up, offensive-minded, but could also put the big hit on guys. I know in that series against Montreal, he stood Beliveau up a few times at center ice. And Jean didn't want to come through the middle again. And Frank Mahovlich would never make a run down that left side – Pierre played right defense – when he was on the ice. He'd always swing into the middle because he didn't want anything to do with Pierre. Pierre was 180 pounds, but solid as can be."

Leading the troops was third-year coach Rudy Pilous. He came from the motivational school of leading rather than the strategic approach.

"Rudy kept us in stitches by the way he talked and by some of his sayings," Mikita said. "He'd always have something to say in the dressing room, 'Jayzus Key-ryst, Nesterenko, if this rink was 14 miles square, you'd be in every corner.' He always gave shit to somebody. But Rudy, and coach Billy Reay as well, always gave shit to Bobby Hull and (me) as well. In fact, he'd target us to deliver a message. We'd be walking out of the dressing room after Rudy took a layer off Bobby and I'd ask Bobby 'Are you OK with that?' Bobby would say, 'yeah, Rudy's just trying to fire us up.' And it would work.

"Rudy wouldn't teach us much as to what we should know about hockey, but he had a way of putting things. When it came time for a power play, he'd say 'OK, I want five guys who can go out there a score a goal.' He made it sound pretty basic."

What shocked Hawk players the most was more Cups didn't follow. And with that came regrets.

"I was too young to appreciate how very important it was going to be," Hull said. "This was going to be one of many that we were going to win. And I didn't even drink out of the Cup. That's how sure I was that this was going to be one of many."

No. 24

1998-99 DALLAS STARS

Foot in the crease or not, Brett Hull's overtime goal gave the Stars the 1998–99 Stanley Cup over Dominik Hasek and the Sabres.

MIKE KEANE CALLS THE 1998-99 DALLAS STARS the most fun he has had in hockey.

Not the best team (although it might be). Not the biggest accomplishment (that's probably the 1993 Montreal Canadiens). But the most fun.

"It was a really great group of guys who came together at the right time," Keane said. "It was as close a team as I have ever been on."

There was talent on the 1999 Stanley Cup champions, but even more impressive, there were characters. Brett Hull, Ed Belfour, Craig Ludwig, Guy Carbonneau… Mike Keane. Mix in a coaching staff led by Ken Hitchcock and a rock solid foundation in character led by GM Bob Gainey and you do have an interesting brew.

"What was great about that team was it was something interesting every day," Ludwig said. "We could have fights in practice, just dig at each other in the locker room and then have a party that same night. But no matter what happened, we all showed up ready to play. That's what I loved about that team, you didn't have to tell anybody how important the games were."

In building the Stars, Gainey trusted his instincts and his past. Gainey knew the Stars scouts had created a great base in drafted players such as Mike Modano, Derian Hatcher, Richard Matvichuk, Jamie Langenbrunner, Jere Lehtinen and Roman Turek. But how do you supplement that?

Well, the first step was getting a little bit of money to spend. The Stars were a financial mess back in 1995 and the lockout didn't help former owner Norman Green. So, when the Stars survived a long dance with John Spano and still didn't have a new owner, things looked pretty grim. But Tom Hicks rode to the rescue and within a month provided the capital for the Stars to make a trade for Joe Nieuwendyk, who was holding out in Calgary with a contract dispute. The price – a prospect named Jarome Iginla – was steep, but the infusion of cash allowed Gainey to trust his instincts while adding what was needed.

"There are so many people who are responsible for this, and everyone knows how much Bob and Ken and the players all did," said former Stars president Jim Lites, "but Tom Hicks meant as much to that championship as anybody else. Without him as the owner, Bob never would have had the chance to make the decisions he did."

And Gainey made some impressive decisions. After making the Nieuwendyk trade, Gainey took a chance on two defensemen who weren't fitting in with their current teams. In retrospect, the deals to get Darryl Sydor and Sergei Zubov in 1996 were steals, but at the time they made sense. Sydor had lost all of his confidence in Los Angeles, so getting both Shane Churla and Doug Zmolek in exchange made sense for the Kings. Zubov didn't understand what Mario Lemieux wanted in Pittsburgh, so having a veteran like Kevin Hatcher on the Penguins seemed like a great decision.

But what Gainey and assistant coach Rick Wilson saw in Sydor and Zubov were two guys with tremendous skill who were in need of confidence boosts. So the two were combined and told to lead the Stars...and they did just that.

The pair was given the chance to play 23 minutes a game, most of the time with Nieuwendyk's line. That left the shutdown pair of Hatcher and Matvichuk to support a line that was learning to play great defense (led by Modano and Lehtinen). It was an important alignment that would help carry Dallas for several years and showed just a little of Hitchcock's genius.

As much as he wanted Modano to score (and Modano led the team in scoring almost every season), Hitchcock wanted even more. He wanted Modano to defend against the other teams' best players.

"We knew Mike had tremendous skills and we needed to find a way to get him out on the ice more," Hitchcock said. "So instead of protecting him, we challenged him to be our best player in every regard...and he responded very well."

Hitchcock seemed to know what to do with every player. Gainey went out and spent big money to acquire a huge free agent goal scorer in Pat Verbeek and then added another right-handed goal scorer a few years later in Brett Hull. Hitchcock put Hull with Modano and forced him to play defense, while he moved Verbeek to a line with Guy Carbonneau and Keane – plenty of grit to go with Verbeek's scoring. Gainey found a veteran check-er in Dave Reid, but Hitchcock used him on a top scoring line with Nieuwendyk and Langenbrunner. Every line seemed to have some offensive ability and a defensive conscience. Even the third defensive pair of Ludwig and Shawn Chambers was more balanced than most knew.

"People knew their roles, but everybody also knew they could do more," Ludwig said. "If Mike Modano was going to play defense, then everybody had to play defense. If Carbo or Keane could come up with a big goal, then everybody had to look to be able to score."

That helped pull the team together. Hull had plenty of ego, but he checked it so he could win the Stanley Cup. Belfour had all sorts of issues, but he curbed them to prove he could win the big one. Players like Verbeek and Chambers accepted lesser roles, because they knew the talent in the room was significant.

"Even when we were at practice, you knew it was a special group," Verbeek said. "Players know that and you understand when you have a real chance to win it all...That said, there were a couple of pretty special teams back then."

Getting past those other special teams in the West was an incredible challenge and the Stars learned that in the 1998 playoffs. They earned the Presidents' Trophy with 109 points and had the highest goal differential at plus-75. However, Nieuwendyk was injured by Bryan Marchment in the first round of the playoffs and Dallas lost in six games to Detroit in the conference final.

In 1999, the challenge was just as great. Dallas again won the Presidents' Trophy (this time with 114 points), but Colorado knocked off the Red Wings in the conference semifinal and had a 3-2 edge on Dallas heading into Game 6 in Denver. And as if on cue, Dallas rode one of its most aggressive games to a 4-1 win as they put 40 shots on goal against Patrick Roy. Jamie Langenbrunner scored twice and Jere Lehtinen and Richard Matvichuk once each. It was the ultimate sign of the team concept.

"I think when we got through that one, there was no way we were going to lose Game 7," Modano said. "It just felt like we were on a mission."

The Stars responded with a 4-1 win in Game 7 at home and moved on to the Cup final.

"WE COULD HAVE FIGHTS IN PRACTICE, JUST DIG AT EACH OTHER IN THE LOCKER ROOM AND THEN HAVE A PARTY THAT SAME NIGHT. BUT NO MATTER WHAT HAPPENED, WE ALL SHOWED UP READY TO PLAY.

– CRAIG LUDWIG

They probably took the Sabres too lightly, losing Game 1 at home, but they then rallied and pulled off the victory in Game 6 when Brett Hull scored a controversial goal in triple overtime.

Hull's skate was in the crease, but the Stars to this day believe the refs made an accurate call to allow the goal. Earlier in the playoffs, Pat Verbeek had a goal disallowed with a skate in the crease and GM Bob Gainey felt the call was wrong. Gainey researched the rule and found an exception where a player could indeed have a skate in the crease if he had control of the puck. Control of the puck, they contended, even extended to retrieving a rebound.

"The rule was very clear and we brought it to the league's attention during the playoffs," Gainey said at the time. "I think it helped that we had already had that discussion and that the league was well aware of how the rule was written."

From the Stars' point of view, it was another sign they had done everything they could to get every break to fall their way. In a lot of ways, the biggest strength of the 1999 Dallas Stars was trust and belief. Everybody in the organization trusted and believed in Gainey, so when he made a statement or a trade, there was no second-guessing. And when the players started to buck Hitchcock's restrictive system, Gainey had his back every time.

"Bob's presence was everywhere," Nieuwendyk said. "It filtered through the entire organization and it was important to all of us. I think it really helped keep us calm at times."

In fact, it probably gave Hitchcock the time he needed to eventually trust his players.

"It was a learning experience for me," Hitchcock said. "And I think a big key was the give and take between the players and the coaches. I was very demanding, we all were. And we wanted to push the players. Because of that, there was a time when they pushed back. But I think what happened that season is the players bought in and took over. They came to us and said, 'We understand, we've got it and we know what to do.'

"When that happened, there was a lot of trust that was built. It was more us accomplishing something together, rather than the coaches pushing or pulling the players. It was a pretty special feeling."

In fact, one of the most special.

"We'll always be linked together by that," Ludwig said. "No matter where you go or how old you are, you can call one of those guys and relive the memories. That was a great team, but even more it was a great bunch of guys."

No. 25

1939-40 NEW YORK RANGERS

Goaltender Dave Kerr, who played 327 of his 427 NHL games with the Rangers, took home the Vezina Trophy for his efforts in 1939–40.

JUST LIKE THE LINGO OF THE TIME, Rangers hockey was something to behold during the 1939-40 season.

And if Blueshirts fans were told in spring of '40 their boys wouldn't win another Stanley Cup for 54 years, it would have caused a real *hoo-ha* on Broadway. The Rangers were *killer-diller* that season and won three Cups and went to three other finals in their first 14 NHL seasons.

GM Lester Patrick – of the famed Patrick family of hockey royalty – had been the Rangers' coach and GM since the club entered the NHL in 1926. And the team he built was *aces.*

Just two of the players on the '39-40 squad, netminder Dave Kerr and captain Art Coulter, were developed by other NHL teams, although some were signed out of senior hockey. And, of course, GM Patrick employed a couple of his own boys, too: sons Lynn and Muzz.

The collection was one of the best to play on Broadway, full of *rip-snorting* forwards, a *raunchy* group of blueliners and a *doozy* of a goalie.

"They actually had three good lines," said Ernie Fitzsimmons of the Society for International Hockey Research. "You take the Colvilles – Mac and Neil, Bryan Hextall, Dutch Hiller, Lynn Patrick, Alf Pike, Alex Shibicky, Kilby MacDonald and Phil Watson all had a fair number of points.

"They had a tough defense, too. Art Coulter was pretty hard to get around. Ott Heller was pretty steady; he scored some. Muzz was a steady, stay-at-home guy; nobody would fight him because he was a boxer...nobody fooled with him."

Hextall, who Fitzsimmons said had a great shot, won the NHL's goal-scoring title that season with 24 in 48 games; his 39 points were good for sixth overall. Watson was the team's premier playmaker – he finished second in the league in assists – and was a regular shift-disturber; think Sean Avery with hands or Ken Linseman during his heyday.

THE COLLECTION WAS ONE OF THE BEST TO PLAY ON BROADWAY, FULL OF *RIP-SNORTING* FORWARDS, A *RAUNCHY* GROUP OF BLUELINERS AND A *DOOZY* OF A GOALIE.

"Watson was a guy who just never gave up – a needler and an agitator, an irritator," Fitzsimmons said. "He was the type of guy everyone on the ice wanted to kill and he could somehow deviate away and set up plays."

Four of those Rangers skaters – Neil Colville, Coulter, Hextall and Lynn Patrick – were later elected to the Hockey Hall of Fame as players, as was their coach, former star Frank Boucher.

The man between the pipes for the Blueshirts was Dave Kerr, who is the lone Ranger to appear on the cover of *TIME* magazine, doing so in 1938. Kerr played every minute of every game for the Blueshirts in '39-40 and led the league with a 1.54 goals-against average and eight shutouts.

"NOBODY WOULD FIGHT HIM BECAUSE HE WAS A BOXER...NOBODY FOOLED WITH HIM."

– HOCKEY HISTORIAN ERNIE FITZSIMMONS ON MUZZ PATRICK

"It was his career season," Fitzsimmons said. "Very impressive."

The '39-40 season was Boucher's first behind the Blueshirts bench; he took over from Patrick after the GM decided to step back from double duty. A former star player, Boucher was also a *slap-happy* coach, a real *fringer* if you asked around. He tried all kinds of new strategies and techniques to gain the upper hand in games.

Boucher has been credited with creating the four-man 'box defense,' now employed around the world by teams killing penalties, and for being the first coach to pull the goalie when trailing during the dying minutes of a game.

As the story goes, the first time Boucher pulled Kerr was against Chicago and nobody knew what was happening. GM Patrick's screams of alarm concerning the *boondoggle* alerted both the Black Hawks and the referee, who blew the play dead out of sheer confusion.

Boucher's innovations seemed to go over well with his players, who clicked as a group all season long.

"I don't think if you take the body of the team that they were any better than anyone else," Fitzsimmons said. "It's just the way he had them playing."

Innovation involving the Rangers wasn't limited just to game play that season. On Feb. 25, 1940, NBC beamed the first televised U.S. hockey game, from New York's Madison Square Garden to the 300 TVs in the Big Apple area. The Rangers beat the Canadiens 6-2 that night, extending their home winning streak to 14 contests (a record that still stands today).

KERR PLAYED EVERY MINUTE OF EVERY GAME FOR THE BLUESHIRTS IN '39-40 AND LED THE LEAGUE WITH A 1.54 GOALS-AGAINST AVERAGE AND EIGHT SHUTOUTS.

Speaking of monumental moments involving the Rangers and the Canadiens: Earlier in the season, the visiting New Yorkers bested the Habs at the Montreal Forum, beginning a record 15-game home winless streak for hockey's greatest franchise.

The Rangers were a great team in '39-40, with two streaks of note. The first was a 17-3-0 run that included a still-standing accomplishment of 10 straight wins and a 19-1-3 streak that cemented a second-overall finish for the Blueshirts.

In the playoffs, the Rangers played the dreaded Boston Bruins in the semifinal. Boston was the defending Cup champ, had posted the top record in the league three consecutive seasons and boasted a veritable murderers' row of forwards.

Milt Schmidt, Woody Dumart, Bobby Bauer and Bill Cowley are all Hall of Famers and took four of the top five spots in the scoring race that season. Schmidt, Dumart and Bauer were collectively known as the 'Kraut Line' and became the first teammates — let alone linemates — to finish 1-2-3 in scoring.

But after both teams received byes to the semifinal, New York, behind Kerr's three shutouts, held Boston's offense in check with the Bruins managing just nine goals in six games.

With the series victory, New York headed to the Cup final to play the Toronto Maple Leafs, who had beaten Chicago and the Detroit Red Wings to reach their third straight championship series and seventh in nine years.

Games 1 and 2 were held at The Garden and the Rangers won both contests to take an early lead in the best-of-seven series. But then, as was the case in those days, the circus came to town — literally. The Blueshirts were forced from The Garden for the remainder of the final so the Ringling Bros. and Barnum & Bailey Circus could set up shop for its annual run; the next five games were set for Toronto's Maple Leaf Gardens.

Not surprisingly, the Leafs won the next two games on home ice before the Blueshirts were able to eke out a 2-1 double-overtime victory in Game 5. The stage was set for a Cup presentation and the Rangers obliged with a 3-2 overtime triumph, handing the Leafs a Cup-final loss for the third straight year.

Watson totaled three goals and nine points in 12 games and Kerr finished with a 1.56 GAA in the post-season. The Conn Smythe Trophy had yet to be minted, but SIHR named Watson its playoff MVP when doing historical awards.

"He led the playoffs in points, but there was more to it than that," Fitzsimmons argued. "We broke it down and he was in on the key goals in three or four of the games along the way.

"He was a constant force and, of course, there was that needling and irritating way he had."

MacDonald won the Calder Trophy as the league's top rookie and Kerr the Vezina for allowing the fewest goals against. Hextall and Kerr were both named first all-stars; Neil Colville, Coulter and coach Boucher made the second team.

A *bananas* dynasty seemed to be in the offing, but instead fans got *bupkis*. The Rangers – and the league – were about to fall on hard times. The Second World War was raging and many top players began putting down their sticks for rifles and heading overseas to fight.

"That was kind of neat," Fitzsimmons said. "Because just before all these guys went to war, they all seemed to hit their peak."

Within two seasons, the Rangers were decimated by enlistment and money problems, making it difficult to compete. By the end of the 1942-43 season, the Blueshirts were the worst team in the NHL, finishing last overall four consecutive years and missing the playoffs 11 of the next 13 seasons.

After showing so much promise in '39-40, the Rangers were never the same, even somewhat tarnishing coach Boucher's hockey legacy.

"Right after (the Stanley Cup win), all the players went to war and Boucher looked like a doughhead because he didn't win anything…he had nothing to work with," Fitzsimmons said.

A fact that would have Rangers fans cursing *dagnabbit* for 54 years after that oh-so-long-ago 1940 Cup.

BEST OF THE REST

AMERICAN LEAGUE

1987-88 HERSHEY BEARS

RIGHT FROM THE TIME THE HOCKEY DEPARTMENT began assembling the Hershey Bears' roster in the summer of 1987, the 50th anniversary season for the storied American League franchise was meant to be special.

The executives from Hershey Entertainment did everything possible to build an American League powerhouse. So, too, did the parent Philadelphia Flyers and their GM, Bob Clarke.

In a place where chocolate is king, failure is not accepted when the Bears set out to do something on a grand scale. This Bears team had everything. There were talented veteran scorers, like forwards Ross Fitzpatrick, Mark Lofthouse and Mitch Lamoureux. There were youngsters the Flyers were anxious to see develop, like wingers Nick Kypreos, Brian Dobbin and Glen Seabrooke.

Plus there were quality veterans to fill roles and teach the kids, like forwards Don Nachbaur, Al Hill and Kevin Maxwell. Wendell Young was deemed the perfect replacement for Ron Hextall, whose AHL apprenticeship would be ending.

The defense had veteran poise and grit from Kevin McCarthy, Dave Fenyves and Steve Smith, plus enthusiasm from prospects Gord Murphy, Jeff Chychrun and John Stevens.

And of course there was toughness.

"Wherever you win, you have to have that mix," Fenyves said.

When the season began, that perfect mix all added up to…a 3-7 start. Ugh.

So much for those grand plans. Management was angry, too.

"I remember being in a hotel room in Utica and getting a call from Clarkey," recalled John Paddock, the team's coach. "We were expected to win and we weren't. He said, 'this is a better team than that. You better get this team going.' "

By late May, all the Bears did was win. They finished the regular season with a then team-record 50 victories. 'Fifty for fifty' was the rally cry as the regular season was winding down.

"It didn't matter who was out there on the ice, you had confidence in them," Fenyves said.

When the playoffs began, the Bears grew even more confident. They rattled off 12-straight playoff wins, becoming the first AHL team in history to sweep their way to a Calder Cup championship.

Three series, three identical 4-0 sweeps – dominating the Binghamton Whalers, the Adirondack Red Wings and, finally, the Fredericton Express. The feat remains unmatched.

"I didn't think much of it during the playoffs," Paddock said, "but for me, not losing a game becomes more special as time goes on."

Paddock sometimes plays the what-if game, though. What if Ray Allison hadn't returned from Europe to play nine playoff games? What if Hershey's veteran scoring star Tim Tookey hadn't been claimed in the waiver draft on the eve of the regular-season opener? What if the Flyers hadn't used their free waiver-draft selection – teams losing a player were allowed to take one – and claimed Fenyves – who was the Calder Cup playoff MVP with the Rochester Americans the year before – from the Buffalo Sabres?

"If we don't lose Tookey, we don't claim 'Fenner,' " Paddock said. "He was just a special player. Without getting Dave…it's all conjecture at this point, but that was a significant starting point for that team. He was so darn good for us."

Tookey had been great for the Bears in the past, though. He was coming off a monster season in 1986-87 when he led the AHL in scoring with 51 goals and 124 points.

"I guess it was more like the NBA thing with (Wilt) Chamberlain and (Bill) Russell," Paddock said. "Wilt won how many scoring championships, but Russell won how many NBA championships?"

There were speed bumps early, however.

"At the beginning of the season we struggled, especially myself," Fenyves said. "I came in late. I remember driving up from Rochester to Sherbrooke (for the season opener) with my dad and then getting there and trying to see where I fit in."

It turns out he fit in like he'd been a Bear for a decade. Midway through the season, Hershey lost captain Don Nachbaur, a rugged, grinding winger who never met a collision he didn't like. He was a prototypical Broad Street Bully, which is why he wore the captain's 'C' for the Bears and why he was called up to the Flyers mid-way through the regular season.

When Nachbaur went up, Paddock transferred the captaincy to Fenyves.

Nachbaur stayed in the NHL right into the Stanley Cup playoffs, though the post-season didn't last long for Philadelphia. The Flyers were eliminated by the Washington Capitals in the first round.

"Right after that series," Nachbaur recalled, "Clarkey said, 'It's

> ## "I GUESS IT WAS MORE LIKE THE NBA THING WITH (WILT) CHAMBERLAIN AND (BILL) RUSSELL. WILT WON HOW MANY SCORING CHAMPIONSHIPS, BUT RUSSELL WON HOW MANY NBA CHAMPIONSHIPS?"
> – COACH JOHN PADDOCK

up to you, you can go back to Hershey or you can call it a season. I never gave it a second thought. In my mind, I knew we had something special in Hershey.

"I got a ring for it an it's still pretty special."

But when he returned, Paddock made a difficult decision.

"Nachbaur had been my captain for two years, but when he came back down I told him, 'I have to leave the 'C' on Fenner,'" Paddock said. "He had been gone so long; I had to do something that was really hard.

"But when we won the Cup, I told Fenner to let Nachbaur take the Cup first. It was only right that it went to him first."

Nachbaur's recall spared him one of the few premeditated, carefully calculated coaching maneuvers crafted by Paddock that season. There was an odd scheduling quirk that saw the Bears go a week without a game, from Saturday to Saturday. Coming into town would be Fredericton, the AHL's highest-scoring team with a 4.6 goals-per-game average.

"We won the game before that break and I gave them Sunday off," Paddock said, "and then I skated them hard for three days. It was like we were in a seven-game losing streak. We did a no-puck skate one day. I remember Kevin McCarthy breaking his stick on the glass.

"But I wanted them really hungry to beat Fredericton."

Needless to say, the Bears won. It was close on the scoreboard, 3-2, but only because Express goalie Ron Tugnutt stopped 48 shots.

The first round series against Binghamton was short and sweet, which, of course, started a trend. The sweep meant the Bears had to wait for their semifinal foe because the Rochester-Adirondack series went seven games.

The year before, the Americans ousted the Bears in five games in the first round. Revenge would have been nice. But deep down, Hershey wanted Adirondack. In 1986, the Red Wings beat the Bears in the Calder Cup final, 4-2.

"There were enough of us left there that we felt we owed them," Paddock said. "They took something from us two years earlier."

Added Nachbaur: "I have some fond memories of that series because the games were wars."

The memories are that much better because the Bears blitzed the Wings in four straight.

By the final, the Bears were simply unstoppable.

"Everyone says, 'Gee, you didn't lose a game, it must have been easy,' " Fenyves said. "There was nothing easy about it."

The season did, however, go exactly according to play.

"We had the exact right amount of what an organization wants," Paddock said. "And when all else failed, Wendell was at the top of his game."

ECHL

2004-05 TRENTON TITANS

IN 12 PROFESSIONAL SEASONS, Rick Kowalsky had never held a championship trophy over his head or sipped champagne from a silver cup.

That all changed in early June 2005.

In the moments after the Trenton Titans had won the ECHL's Kelly Cup by beating the Florida Everblades 4-1 in front of 7,805 fans on the road in Game 6 of the final, Kowalsky was summoned to paste the last piece of a puzzle on the visitors' dressing room wall.

Coach Mike Haviland and assistant Ted Dent had used this postgame ritual as a motivational tool throughout the playoffs. After each victory, a key player was selected to paste one section of the puzzle to the board. There were 14 pieces – the number of wins it would take to win the title. The completed puzzle was a large photo of the Kelly Cup.

As champagne squirted throughout the room and players and coaches hooted and hollered, Kowalsky, sporting a healthy playoff beard and wearing a Titans Kelly Cup championship cap, took the final puzzle piece, peeled off the tape on the back of the plaque and prepared to put it in place. He fought back tears as he addressed the team.

"That man called me over a year ago; he said, 'I want you to win a championship,' " said Kowalsky, rubbing his hand across his face while trying to keep his emotions in check as he pointed to Haviland. "I put my belief in him because I know what type of person he is and I know what type of coach he is. We're standing here and we're champions. No one will ever take what we did away, ever."

The 2004-05 Titans earned The Hockey News' pick as the Greatest Team in ECHL History by beating four playoff teams that had finished the regular season with 92 or more points: Atlantic City (92 points); Reading (93); Alaska (98); and Florida (94).

Trenton traveled more than 4,000 miles to Anchorage, Alaska – twice – in order to win the National Conference final. Next was a long trek south to Naples, Fla., for the championship series against the Florida Everblades.

Trenton's championship came during the NHL's 2004-05 lockout. Many AHL-caliber players competed in the ECHL that season. A few NHL players also skated on ECHL ice, most notably Alaska's Scott Gomez.

"That team, early on in the summer in recruiting, I got Rick Kowalsky, a proven winner at that level and a veteran captain," said Haviland. "That's what I felt we needed in the organization to lead the team."

Scott Bertoli, a prolific scorer, had been with the Titans since the team formed in 1999. Andrew Allen was a proven goaltender. Depth came from players such as Les Haggett, Nick Deschenes, Paul Brown, Tim Judy, Steve Munn, Rosario Ruggeri, Leon Hayward and Jarrett Thompson.

"I PUT MY BELIEF IN HIM BECAUSE I KNOW WHAT TYPE OF PERSON HE IS AND I KNOW WHAT TYPE OF COACH HE IS. WE'RE STANDING HERE AND WE'RE CHAMPIONS. NO ONE WILL EVER TAKE WHAT WE DID AWAY, EVER."

– RICK KOWALSKY

"Mike Haviland had done a good job of bringing in a good group of older guys," said Bertoli, who played eight seasons with Trenton. "We knew what his expectations were. We knew he was a great coach and he knew how to deal with different personalities."

Kowalsky, who had been coerced to rejoin Trenton after playing the three previous seasons with the ECHL's Roanoke Express, was the '05 Titans captain and emotional leader.

"That team was special," said Kowalsky, now Trenton's coach. "We were and may still be the only team in the history of the ECHL to have to play four rounds against teams that had 90-plus point seasons. It was the lockout year and maybe the deepest and most talented teams this league will ever see. There were at least 10 NHL players in the league. We saw Shane Hnidy in the finals in Florida and Scott Gomez helped Alaska get to the semis.

"Seven of our 20 playoff games went into overtime. We probably broke the record for distance traveled in a playoff run having to go to Alaska and Florida twice each."

There was more.

"The Hockey News picked us to win it before the season and I don't think any team picked has actually gone on and won it," Kowalsky said. "We did not have any superstars. We didn't have one guy that won it for us. We truly were a great team in every sense of the word. The fact that our third line center, Leon Hayward, won the playoff MVP says a lot."

Trenton opened the season with a six-game winning streak and allowed just nine goals. By New Year's Eve, the Titans had a 17-5-4 record. But injuries and call-ups brought Trenton back to reality, including a 3-7-1 January.

"You go through your ups and downs," Haviland said. "We went through a stretch when we were not very good. We learned how to come out of that adversity as a group."

Haviland didn't stand pat either.

"We picked up Jarrett Thompson from Augusta," he said. "And we solidified our defense when we got Steve Munn from Augusta.

"I signed Les Haggett out of Brown and Tim Judy out of Northeastern. Flyers (GM) Paul Holmgren was extremely helpful. We had Nick Deschenes and T.J. Robinson. Another key was that I had a good relationship with Claude Noel, who was with Nashville and Milwaukee. We got Paul Brown on loan when Milwaukee got knocked out of the playoffs."

Trenton finished the regular season at 42-21-9 and tied rival Reading with 93 points in the North Division.

The Titans opened the playoffs against Atlantic City, the team Haviland coached to the Kelly Cup two years earlier. Trenton swept the best-of-five series, but needed overtime in Games 2 and 3. Reading had home-ice in the division final and won Game 1. Trenton took the next three, in one-goal games, and the series.

That set up a hastily arranged voyage to Anchorage for the National Conference final.

"We had two different planes because we couldn't get everybody on one plane," Haviland said.

The hectic schedule took a toll as the Aces humbled the Titans 6-0 in the opener. But in what might have been the key to the title run, Trenton came back to win 7-1 in Game 2.

"We got absolutely clocked in Game 1 and then turned around and beat them in Game 2," Bertoli remembered.

The series went the distance with Trenton winning Game 7 in Alaska.

"We were home for a day; we turned around and went to Florida," Bertoli said of the 1,227-mile trip to Naples.

The Titans' road success continued as Trenton had an unlikely two-game sweep in Florida. With the next three games in Trenton, the Titans prepared to claim the Cup on home ice. But Florida won twice.

"We had a stranglehold," Bertoli said. "We came home and got a little ahead of ourselves. We lost Game 3 in overtime and lost Game 4. It was a tied series. We were trailing in Game 5. Then the turning point of the series was when we dominated the third period of Game 5.

"We outscored them 5-0 in that period and I don't think the puck left their zone. That was one of the most dominating performances I had seen at any level by any team."

The Titans clinched the Kelly Cup during the next game in Florida.

"We, as a team, the leadership we had in the room with Kowalsky, Vince Williams, Matt Libby, Bertoli, Hayward and Haviland...there was never a sense of panic no matter what happened in the playoffs," said Allen, who had 30 regular-season wins and all 14 playoff wins. "There was never a panic. There was calm when Haviland walked into the room. It all started with him and Teddy Dent, our assistant coach."

QUEBEC LEAGUE

1970-71 QUEBEC REMPARTS

ANDRE SAVARD may have never won a Stanley Cup during his 12-year NHL career with the Boston Bruins, Buffalo Sabres and Quebec Nordiques, but he was part of something special before that.

He was a high-scoring center for the 1970-71 Quebec Remparts, a star-studded group that's THN's choice for the greatest Quebec League team of all-time. It was a club that dominated opponents en route to capturing both the QMJHL championship and Memorial Cup.

"I always felt I was lucky to be in the right place at the right time in junior," Savard said. "There's so many great memories I can reflect on. I still remember everything about that team.

"Guy Lafleur was the big star, but we also had other very good players on that team. Guy was the kind of player that if he had one goal, he wanted two. If he had two, he wanted three. If he had three, he wanted four. He was hungry for success and that rubbed off on our entire team."

With a 54-7-1 record, Quebec finished atop the QMJHL and posted a league record .879 winning percentage. The club finished ahead of its nearest foe, the Shawinigan Bruins, by 32 points — the biggest differential between the top two clubs in league history.

The Remparts led the league in goals for (437) and goals against (205) in the regular season. They were 12-1 in the playoffs and defeated the Edmonton Oil Kings to capture the 1971 Memorial Cup in Quebec City.

The Remparts were led by Lafleur, who won the QMJHL scoring title with 130 goals and 209 points in 62 games. The club's top five point producers were rounded out by Michel Briere (144), Savard (139), Jacques Richard (113) and Richard Grenier (99).

"We were a talented team, but also very hard working," Savard said. "Maurice Filion was a coach who was very demanding. He expected a lot from his team. It was run like a professional team in every sense.

"I remember in the playoffs the box office opened at 9 a.m. and fans were waiting in line for tickets 15 hours before. All the games were sellouts. It was an incredible atmosphere at Le Colisee de Quebec."

Quebec was a powerful offensive machine that scored an average of 7.04 goals per game. Nobody else in the league averaged five per game that season.

That club still owns the QMJHL record for fewest losses in a season and finished with 109 points. It played 10 less games than 1978-79 Trois Rivieres, which owns the league record with 122 points.

"They were dominant in every aspect of the game," said former Rosemont National defenseman Clement Jodoin. "They had size, strength, toughness, speed and they were loaded with skill. They had everything. They had no weaknesses. It was no surprise for me when they won the Memorial Cup."

Jodoin had front row seats the night in 1970-71 when Savard set the QMJHL record with 12 points in a 14-1 win over Rosemont.

"THEY WERE DOMINANT IN EVERY ASPECT OF THE GAME. THEY HAD SIZE, STRENGTH, TOUGHNESS, SPEED AND THEY WERE LOADED WITH SKILL. THEY HAD EVERYTHING. THEY HAD NO WEAKNESSES. IT WAS NO SURPRISE FOR ME WHEN THEY WON THE MEMORIAL CUP."
– FORMER ROSEMONT NATIONAL DEFENSEMAN CLEMENT JODOIN

"I remember being on the ice for a few of those goals," said Jodoin with a laugh. "I'm not sure how many."

QMJHL commissioner Gilles Courteau has vivid memories of that Quebec squad.

"The Remparts were the biggest franchise in the CHL at the time, averaging 10,000 fans per game," he said. "They were a leader in so many ways. They were the first CHL franchise to have a full-time marketing person.

"The atmosphere in the building was amazing. That was an out-standing team, very spectacular to watch. Everywhere they went they drew big crowds. It was the league's second season and they helped us gain credibility by winning the Memorial Cup."

Two honorable mentions for greatest all-time QMJHL club are the 1995-96 Granby Predateurs and 2004-05 Rimouski Oceanic.

Granby was 56-12-2 in the regular season and ended the league's 14-year drought by capturing the 1996 Memorial Cup. Rimouski, led by Sidney Crosby, posted a league record 35-game undefeated (regular season and playoff) streak to end the season, but wound up losing in the 2005 Memorial Cup final.

Quebec's 1970-71 squad stands out most due to its degree of dominance and the impact it had on the pros. It boasted four 100-point producers and four 50-goal scorers.

That edition of the Remparts developed future NHLers in Lafleur, Savard, Grenier, Richard and Gilles Lupien and also several others who played minor pro.

It was a club that registered 54 wins, the fourth most in league history, and it achieved this in just 62 games. The league record of 58 wins is shared by 1978-79 Trois Rivieres Draveurs (72 games) and 1973-74 Sorel Black Hawks (70 games).

Quebec held a 3-1 series lead on the St. Catharines Black Hawks of the Ontario League in the 1971 Memorial Cup final. Game 4 in Quebec City ended in a major brawl and the Black Hawks had to be escorted through an angry mob of fans back to their bus.

Game 5 was moved to Maple Leaf Gardens in Toronto to avoid a repeat ugly incident and Quebec lost, cutting its series lead to 3-2. The Black Hawks refused to return to Quebec City for the next game and the Remparts were handed the trophy.

Quebec wanted to capture the Memorial Cup in a more honorable way, so it challenged Western League champion Edmonton. The Remparts swept the best-of-three series with 5-1 and 5-2 victories.

"Our team was controlling the game from start to finish," Lupien said. "We were so powerful that every team was trying to in-timidate us. They were trying to fight because they didn't know any other way to play against us. They knew they couldn't play hockey with us.

"When Guy Lafleur was going on the ice, he had two goals right away. Same thing for Andre Savard. We had so much talent, but we also had lots of size, toughness and we were strong defensively."

ONTARIO LEAGUE

2004-05 LONDON KNIGHTS

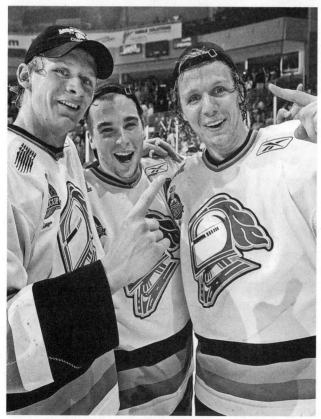

Corey Perry, Dylan Hunter, Marc Methot and the rest of the London Knights capped a remarkable season with a 4–0 win in the Memorial Cup final over Rimouski

TINA TURNER'S "Simply The Best" fits the 2004-05 Memorial Cup champion London Knights. It's not a stretch to proclaim the team is the best in Ontario League history and perhaps even

Canadian League history, but that's a debate for another book. Let the facts speak:

The '04-05 Knights just didn't rewrite the record book, they dismantled it as they celebrated their first OHL and Memorial Cup championships in their 40-year history. And it came almost five years to the date the franchise was bought by brothers Dale and Mark Hunter in 2000.

Four years prior to the Hunters, the Knights were the worst team in CHL history with a dreadful 3-60-3 record in 1995-96.

The Hunters had set 2005 as the year to win – and it helped when they gained an automatic berth in the Memorial Cup a year earlier when London won the right to host the tournament.

During training camp in August, Corey Perry said there would be no back door for the Knights; they were going in the front door. But nobody expected them to bash it down like they did.

There was no NHL that season; the league had locked out its players. So the Canadian media turned to major junior for its hockey fix and when the Knights got off to a 31-game unbeaten streak to start, the team was thrust into the national spotlight.

"It's fitting that in their 40th year they be recognized as one of the greatest teams to ever play," said OHL commissioner and CHL president David Branch. "And that record is not just about wins, it's about the way the London Knights hockey club captured the attention of the entire country.

Added Mark Hunter, the team's GM: "I think the kids enjoyed the attention and I think that went a long ways towards making them good. They enjoyed everyone talking about what they accomplished. Some teams you watch and you worry about outside pressure, but these kids, I honestly think, survived on it."

Hunter said it helped a player like Perry, who became the Knights' all-time points leader that season, come out of his shell and evolve into the dominant NHLer he has become.

"I think it was always in him, it just took something like that to bring it out of him and we saw how he thrived in that situation," Hunter said. "He's a true winner."

Perry said the season was special for so many reasons, but most memorable for him was the way the group came together.

CHL RECORDS

Best winning percentage: .882 (59-7-2-0, 120 points).
Previous: .879, Quebec Remparts (54-7-1), 1970-71.
Longest undefeated streak: 31 games (29-0-2-0).
Previous: 29 games (24-0-5), Brandon Wheat Kings, 1978-79.
Longest undefeated streak to start a season: 31 games (29-0-2-0).
Previous: 29 games (24-0-5), Brandon, 1978-79.
Fewest goals against: 125.
Previous: 125, Kelowna Rockets, 2003-04.
Most records in a season: four.
Previous: four, Shawinigan Dynamos, 1977-78; Brandon, 1978-79.

OHL RECORDS

Most wins: 59.
Previous: 54, Sault Ste. Marie Greyhounds, 1984-85.
Most points: 120.
Previous: 110, London, 2003-04.
First team with back-to-back 50-win seasons.
First team with back-to-back 100-point seasons.
Fewest losses: seven.
Previous: seven, Toronto Marlboros, 1972-73.
Fewest road losses: six.
Previous: seven, Oshawa Generals, 1990-91; Ottawa 67's, 1998-99.
Best winning percentage: .882 (59-7-2-0).
Previous: .826, Sault Ste. Marie Greyhounds (54-11-1), 1984-85.
Longest undefeated streak: 31 games (29-0-2-0).
Previous: 25 games (25-0-0), Kitchener Rangers, 1983-84.
Longest undefeated streak to start a season: 31 games (29-0-2-0).
Previous: 11, Kitchener, 1981-82 (10-0-1); Windsor Spitfires, 1986-87 (10-0-1). Peterborough Petes, 1992-93 (11-0-0); Guelph Storm, 1995-96 (11-0-0).
Most road wins: 28.
Previous: 24, Ottawa, 1998-99; Guelph, 2003-04.
Longest road winning streak: 14 games.
Previous: 11, Kitchener, 1983-84.
Longest road undefeated streak: 14 games.
Previous: 12, Oshawa, 1982-83.
Fewest goals against: 125.
Previous: 147, London, 2003-04.
Best goals-against average: 1.70, Gerald Coleman.
Previous: 2.06, Ryan MacDonald, London, 2003-04.
Most team shutouts: 13.
Previous: 10, Ottawa, 1997-98.
Most OHL records in a season: 15.
Previous: six, Sault Ste. Marie, 1984-85.

"Everybody just gathered around each other and all the records just kind of evolved," he said. "After going undefeated in 31 games, we decided we had a chance to do something special.

"It's something that obviously helped get me ready for the next level. But you have to look at how many guys on that team are playing in the NHL on a regular basis or have played in the NHL (11 as of May 2010) and that's just crazy.

"A lot of guys got an opportunity to prove themselves and it just goes to show how good the Hunters are at developing players."

While the records continued to fall, the players weren't preoccupied with taking their place in history. On a lot of nights, they had to be informed of their latest entry.

"THIS TEAM WENT 31 GAMES WITHOUT A LOSS. THAT IS A HELL OF AN ACCOMPLISHMENT. USUALLY THERE'S A LETDOWN AFTER SOMETHING LIKE THAT, BUT THIS TEAM JUST KEPT PLUGGING ALONG AND THE DRIVE TO SUCCEED WAS HUGE.

– GM MARK HUNTER

"It was interesting," Perry said. "We just loved hockey and enjoyed going out and winning every night."

And there was that issue of not sneaking into Memorial Cup, but getting in as league champs.

"We could have taken the easy way out, but we talked as a team and Dale and the coaching staff really helped get us where we wanted to go," Perry said. "They didn't let our heads get too big."

Dale Hunter's coaching method was simple, said Perry.

"If you weren't going to play the way he wanted you to, you would sit," he said. "I know. I missed a couple shifts. It showed he had full control of the hockey team."

Because of the NHL lockout, the Memorial Cup became a media circus. Adding to it was the fact it was Sidney Crosby's draft year and his Rimouski Oceanic were the Quebec League champions. If there was ever a time for the Knights to wilt under the pressure, that would be it.

But again they welcomed the challenge and after going through the round-robin undefeated, met Crosby and the Oceanic in the final – the Knights dominated 4-0, ending the year with a 79-9-2-0 record.

"The Memorial Cup never got more exposure because there was no NHL hockey," Mark Hunter said. "We had the Gary Bettmans there; those kinds of people are not going to show up if there's an NHL. And there was so much hype over Sidney Crosby coming. How huge was the media interest? We had to take out half of our standing room to accommodate the extra media.

"It all comes down to one game and that's why I give the credit to those kids. They were really focused on winning. They could have been distracted, but they weren't."

Despite the impressive start to the season, the GM had done some tweaking, including bringing in goalie Adam Dennis from the Guelph Storm.

"We knew we were going to be hard to beat, but we also knew we needed some depth in the playoffs," he said. "We did a little bit of an upgrade in our goaltending and at the end of the day, Adam was the playoff performer we knew he'd be."

Hunter had played on the 1989 Stanley Cup champion Calgary Flames, but said he's never seen a team as consistent as the '04-05 Knights.

"This team went 31 games without a loss. That is a hell of an accomplishment," he said. "Usually there's a letdown after something like that, but this team just kept plugging along and the drive to succeed was huge.

"Those kids *wanted* to win."

WESTERN LEAGUE

1978-79 BRANDON WHEAT KINGS

IT WAS IN THE SPRING OF 1979 when left winger Brian Propp grabbed a marker and scratched out a challenge on the dressing room wall to all future Brandon Wheat Kings teams.

"125 pts, try to beat that!" Propp wrote.

To this day, no team has.

Propp's words and that record have stood the test of time, as the 1978-79 Wheat Kings remain one of the greatest teams in junior hockey history and still hold Canadian League records for most points (125) and fewest losses (five) in a season.

The Wheat Kings posted a brilliant 58-5-9 record to lead the Western League, with no less than 10 team members drafted by NHL clubs that season – the most ever by a WHL team – including four in the first round alone: center Laurie Boschman (ninth overall to Toronto), Propp (14th overall to Philadelphia), defenseman Brad McCrimmon (15th overall to Boston) and right winger Ray Allison (18th overall to Hartford). Blueliner Mike Perovich (23rd overall to Atlanta) would have also been a first-rounder by today's standards, a testament to the talent assembled that season by GM Jack Brockest and chief scout Ron Dietrich.

But any great team also needs a great leader and the Wheat Kings had one of the best behind the bench in coach Dunc McCallum.

"I think when people think of the '78-79 Wheat Kings, for any of the players that played on it, the first thing they would think about is Dunc McCallum and the leadership and coaching he brought and the respect he had from his players," said Kelly McCrimmon, current coach-GM and owner of the Wheat Kings and a rookie on that historic WHL championship squad. "Add to that the star power and then I think anybody who played against us would say toughness. Dunc had tough teams and the Wheat Kings through those years in the late '70s were a very tough team."

It was a decidedly different era of hockey when the WHL was truly the Wild West. Bench-clearing brawls were the norm and players like Boschman could score 66 goals and still find time to amass 215 penalty minutes. Tim Lockridge and Don Gillen led the way in terms of toughness, but a whopping 12 Wheat Kings piled up more than 100 penalty minutes.

"All I know is not too many teams enjoyed getting into one of those (brawls) with our team," said Propp, who scored 219 goals in 213 career games as a Wheat King and racked up a franchise-record 511 points over three seasons.

Tough but talented, the 1978-79 Wheat Kings boasted a bevy of future NHLers, with Propp (94 goals, 194 points), Allison (60 goals, 153 points) and Boschman (66 goals, 149 points) forming the highest scoring line in WHL history and finishing 1-2-3 in league scoring before moving on to lengthy professional careers.

"The thing that sticks out for me is just how good the good guys were," Kelly McCrimmon said. "Brian Propp had 194 points, he had 94 goals. Brad McCrimmon played 55 minutes a game routinely. He played 58 minutes of the Memorial Cup final … and Ray Allison and Laurie (Boschman), all those guys were such good players."

"THERE HAVE BEEN SOME GREAT TEAMS, BUT WHEN YOU LOOK AT OUR RECORD, WE ONLY LOST FIVE GAMES THAT YEAR AND THAT'S PRETTY AMAZING OVER A 72-GAME SCHEDULE, ESPECIALLY WITH THE WAY WE TRAVELED…IT WAS A PRETTY REMARKABLE SEASON."

– BRIAN PROPP

Remarkably, the Wheat Kings went almost three months without losing a game. Brandon set a CHL record for longest unbeaten streak to start a season at 29 games – a 24-0-5 mark surpassed by 2004-05 Ontario League London Knights with 31 – and the Wheat Kings still hold the CHL record for longest regular season unbeaten streak spanning two seasons at 49 games (Feb. 11, 1978 to Dec. 13, 1978).

"The biggest thing I remember about that year was we would be down in some games or having close games and we just knew we were going to win," said Don Dietrich, a 17-year-old rookie defenseman for the Wheat Kings that season. "You just knew somebody was going to step up and pull it out."

Brandon's unbeaten streak was finally snapped in Edmonton by the Oil Kings on Dec. 13, one night after the Wheat Kings had faced the Moscow Selects in an exhibition game.

After dropping a 9-3 decision to the powerful Soviet touring team – featuring players largely in their mid-20s — the Wheat Kings boarded the bus for an overnight trip to Edmonton. Penalty problems plagued the Wheat Kings that night as the Oil Kings, who won only 17 games that season, struck nine times on the power play – with Ray Neufeld firing four goals – in a 9-4 victory that ended Brandon's streak at 29.

"Edmonton didn't have a very good team," Dietrich said, "but everything they did was right that night."

The Wheat Kings lost only four more games over the course of that season, setting another league record by scoring 491 goals (later topped by the 496 scored by the 1986-87 Kamloops Blazers).

After rolling through the playoffs and capturing the WHL championship by beating the Portland Winter Hawks in six games, the Wheat Kings advanced all the way to the Memorial Cup final in Verdun, Que., before dropping a heartbreaking 2-1 overtime decision to the OHL's Peterborough Petes, the only blemish on an otherwise brilliant season.

"Of course you always wish you would have won a Memorial Cup because that's what a lot of people judge you by," said Propp, who was named the left winger on the CHL's all-time team in 1999. "There have been some great teams, but when you look at our record, we only lost five games that year and that's pretty amazing over a 72-game schedule, especially with the way we traveled…It was a pretty remarkable season.

NCAA

1992-93 MAINE BLACK BEARS

IT WAS A TEAM THAT BY ALL ACCOUNTS, should not have been assembled; the parts too disparate and daunting to put together.

But thanks to coach Shawn Walsh and legendary assistants Grant Standbrook and Dennis 'Red' Gendron, the University of Maine Black Bears rolled out a devastating lineup that ran up a 42-1-2 record and took the 1992-93 national championship.

"It was the greatest recruiting class of all-time," said Anaheim Ducks senior vice-president of hockey operations and former

Paul Kariya averaged 2.56 points per game during his 1992–93 season at the University of Maine.

assistant GM David McNab, a long-time NCAA expert. "That trio was not destined for that school."

'That trio,' was comprised of freshmen Paul Kariya and twin brothers Chris and Peter Ferraro, none of whom call Maine home. But Maine will certainly not forget them.

Kariya, later taken fourth overall by Anaheim in 1993, was a B.C. native who trekked across the continent and immediately laid waste to his NCAA opponents. The fleet-footed left winger put up a remarkable 100 points in 39 games, becoming a rare freshman-winner of the Hobey Baker Memorial Award as college player of the year.

The Ferraro twins of New York were just as tantalizing, especially since one came with the other. Peter was taken 24th overall by the Rangers in 1992, while the Blueshirts also scooped up his brother that year with the 85th selection.

Along with returning scorers Cal Ingraham and Jim Montgomery, that's a lot of talent for just one puck, but the players were committed to making it work. The Ferraros had been playing junior hockey in the Midwest with Dubuque and Waterloo of the United States League and had even talked about staying in the heartland for college, but Maine's program won them over.

"We were so impressed by the powerhouse they had there," said Peter Ferraro, "and the Rangers were very high on the program."

The allure of joining forces with Kariya didn't hurt, either.

"I remember him at the world juniors," Ferraro recalled. "He was so electrifying to watch and I envisioned my brother and I playing with him."

In the end, Kariya played more with Montgomery, but that only served to give Maine two big lines to trot out offensively. Along with Kariya's century mark, Maine got 95 points from Montgomery, 85 from Ingraham and at least 50 from both Ferraros and Mike Latendresse.

"If you have three players with 50 points these days in college, you probably win it all," McNab remarked. "That was their *second* line."

But it wasn't just offense that helped Maine conquer the nation. The Black Bears were also blessed with two future NHL netminders, Garth Snow and Mike Dunham.

Snow is now GM of the New York Islanders, while Dunham is the team's goaltending coach.

"Right from the start," Snow said, "we knew we had a good team."

"I JUST REMEMBER SITTING IN THE ROOM PANICKING, ALMOST CRYING. COACH CAME IN AND SAID WE WERE GOING TO WIN."
– PETER FERRARO

And they didn't take long to get going. In the season opener against Providence, the Bears beat up the Friars 9-3 before tying 3-3 the next day. In the first 24 Hockey East conference games, Maine tallied nearly three times as many goals-for as goals-against (163-56). The one setback came at home to Boston University, a 7-6 overtime loss on Feb. 19 that still stings.

"That feeling…we didn't like it," Ferraro said. "We weren't used to it, but coach Walsh came into the dressing room after and said, 'You know what? I like the loss – it's good for you guys.' "

And the coach would prove to be prophetic. The Bears never lost again that season, even when trailing in some of the most crucial post-season games. At the Frozen Four in Milwaukee, Wisc., the Bears were down to Mike Knuble's Michigan Wolverines and Brian Rolston's Lake Superior State Lakers before pulling out dramatic victories.

The 4-3 overtime win against Michigan in the semifinal was particularly galvanizing for Ferraro. Trailing the Wolverines heading into the third period, he recalled the dressing room during the second intermission.

"I just remember sitting in the room panicking, almost crying," Ferraro said. "Coach came in and said we were going to win."

The same come-from-behind mentality raised its head against the Lakers in the final, with Maine down 4-2 heading into the final frame. Ferraro saw the fire in Kariya's eyes and knew it wasn't over.

"I thought," Ferraro said, " 'we can't lose – we've got this kid in our room. This kid's not going to lose – he won't accept it.'"

And Kariya didn't. He set up Montgomery for three goals as the Bears took their first-ever national championship, 5-4. But Kariya wasn't the only soldier in the trenches.

Snow and Dunham had alternated in net all season long and Dunham started the final. But four Lake Superior goals in the first two periods (including three in the second) chased Dunham and put the Bears in a serious hole; the Lakers had only lost once that season when leading after 40 minutes.

"They seemed to be the best team we had faced at cycling the puck and getting the puck deep," Snow said. "And any team coached by Jeff Jackson is going to be disciplined.

"When coach Walsh put me in, he told me to play every puck and prevent them from cycling it. I took a lot of chances and he gave me the freedom to do that."

The ability of Walsh to get the most out of his players was key to the Bears' success and Ferraro pointed to the coach's strength at knowing the different personalities of all his charges.

"We were a really focused, serious team," he said.

Snow also remembers a squad that bonded very well.

"We were very close-knit," said the former netminder. "We were watching football together on Sundays, playing cards on the road or video games – there was always a setup in someone's room."

But it all came back to Walsh and his ability to coax players from B.C., Quebec, New York and Massachusetts to come to Maine and play for him – not his Hockey East rivals.

In previous campaigns, he served notice that his recruiting was not limited to Maine's state borders, scooping up Bob Corkum (Massachusetts), Dave Capuano (Rhode Island) and Keith Carney (Rhode Island) from other Northeastern locales.

"Shawn had as much an effect on college hockey as anyone," McNab said. "He changed the dynamics across the country. He went toe-to-toe with everyone in the East.

"He woke everybody up."

CANADA

1987 CANADA CUP

EARLY IN THE 1987 Canada Cup tournament, Canadian defenseman Ray Bourque made an observation about his team.

"It's scary," he said at the time. "You see the puck moving around and you can't believe it. It would be scary if you could keep this team together for a whole season."

Scary indeed. The fact is, Canada has assembled more individual talent than the team that won the '87 Canada Cup, but never has it had a better unit, led by two of the greatest players ever to play the game.

Canadian coach Mike Keenan resisted the urge to put Wayne Gretzky and Mario Lemieux together until the second game of the three-game final, but when he did, it affirmed Gretzky's status as the greatest player in the world and Lemieux as the heir apparent.

When Mario Lemieux and Wayne Gretzky were put on the same line during the Canada Cup final against the Soviets it was pure magic.

That's only part of what makes the '87 team the greatest to represent Canada, however. The fact it won the final three-game series against the Soviet Union in a tournament that provided a level of competition that has never been higher goes a long way. The fact Canada had a power play consisting of Gretzky, Lemieux and Mark Messier up front with Paul Coffey and Bourque on defense also plays a factor. The fact Dale Hawerchuk, one of the greatest offensive talents of all-time, played a checking role along with Brent Sutter and Rick Tocchet is a good indicator.

THE THREE 6-5 GAMES IN THE FINAL SERIES, TWO OF WHICH WERE DECIDED IN OVERTIME, WERE CONSIDERED BY MANY TO BE THE BEST THREE GAMES EVER PLAYED.

The 1987 team had (just) 11 players who ultimately made it to the Hall of Fame, compared to 15 on the 1972 Summit Series team, 17 on the 1976 Canada Cup team and 12 on each of the 1981 and 1984 teams. But the '87 team faced a level of competition that was far superior to any of those teams. The Soviet Union was particularly formidable, boasting a top line of Igor Larionov between Vladimir Krutov and Sergei Makarov, three players who could have given Gretzky and Lemieux a challenge had they been playing (all three eventually did play in the NHL later) in the NHL. The three 6-5 games in the final series, two of which were decided in overtime, were considered by many to be the best three games ever played.

Gretzky has since said the tournament was the pinnacle of his career in terms of his level of play and Lemieux, after some expressed concerns about his big-game ability early in his career, led all players with 11 goals and was an unstoppable force.

"I think I answered a few questions in this tournament," Lemieux said after it was over.

What also made the '87 team special was the sum of its parts, not just its superstar players. On defense, Coffey and Bourque were the obvious marquee players, but the two best all-around defensemen for Canada might have been the far-less heralded Normand Rochefort and Doug Crossman, who were assigned the shutdown role and, considering how offensive the game was in that era, did a very good job. Messier, Mike Gartner and Glenn Anderson were assigned the task of going head-to-head with the Soviets' top line.

The tournament was played in an era that was on the cusp of hockey becoming a big-money sport. That makes it the good old days.

"At 30 bucks a pop," Murphy said after the final, alluding to the high cost of tickets, "you want everyone to get their money's worth."

UNITED STATES

1996 WORLD CUP

THE BEST AMERICAN HOCKEY TEAM of all-time didn't need a miracle.

No U.S. team has ever achieved more fame than the 1980 Olympic squad that stunned the Soviet Union in the semifinal before completing the 'Miracle on Ice' by beating Finland for gold in Lake Placid, N.Y.

That squad's spectacular rise is one of the best stories in sports history, period. The reason for that, though, is because it was

Goaltender Mike Richter was never better than he was at the 1996 World Cup.

the ultimate underdog tale, a group – as they've so often been described – of rag-tag college kids shocking the world.

The shock was still there 16 years later at the next big triumph for Team USA, but it was more about how good the team was rather than the fact it took on the world and won.

The American team that beat Canada in a best-of-three final at the 1996 World Cup is the best collection ever to wear stars and stripes. It was a coming out party for Team USA, which rolled through the round-robin, toppled Russia in the semifinal and bounced back from a Game 1 overtime loss in the final to earn consecutive victories over Canada in Montreal to win the tournament previously known as the Canada Cup.

"I'LL NEVER FORGET WALKING TO THE RINK FOR GAME 3 WITH ME, BILLY GUERIN AND DOUG WEIGHT JUST GETTING ABUSED BY FANS UP THERE."

– KEITH TKACHUK

It became America's Cup thanks to a stunning combination of speed and strength contained within a mix of veteran leaders such as Chris Chelios, Brian Leetch and Joel Otto, and an emerging crew of young power forwards such as John LeClair, Bill Guerin, Adam Deadmarsh and Keith Tkachuk. Its brightest star up front was scoring machine Brett Hull, who led all point-getters at the event with seven goals and 11 points and was named to the tournament all-star team.

And don't forget about goalie Mike Richter. As strong as the U.S. was, beating Canada three out of four times in the tournament, including round-robin play, they still needed Richter to play spectacularly before rallying late to win Game 3 by a 5-2 count, the winner coming from the stick of Tony Amonte.

Tkachuk, who had a fantastic tournament for the Americans at age 24, scoring five goals in seven games, gives Richter credit for the big win in the decisive game.

"No question, he won us the game," Tkachuk said. "You need that goaltending. I don't think we played as well as we should have, but he made big saves at the right time and kept us in it."

The final game notwithstanding, the Americans overpowered teams – including Canada – throughout the event. Constructed by GM Lou Lamoriello, they were big, fast and tough, and coach Ron Wilson pushed all the right buttons.

Distraught as Team Canada and Canadian fans were at losing a hockey showdown to their southern neighbors, this was no upset; it was simply a case of one country announcing its presence as the sport's newest superpower.

"I respect this team as much as any team we've ever played in a Canada Cup tournament," said Canadian Mark Messier of the Americans before Game 2 of the final. "This American team, with the program they've put together, it's one of the greatest teams to play in international competition."

And demonstrating just how good they were in Canada in front of the rabid Canuck fans was particularly sweet for the victorious Americans.

"I'll never forget walking to the rink for Game 3 with me, Billy Guerin and Doug Weight just getting abused by fans up there," Tkachuk said. "It was so packed outside the rink before the game. And then to come back and win and go outside the rink, it was a ghost town. I think everybody couldn't believe what happened."

RUSSIA

1983 WORLD CHAMPIONSHIP

TAKE THE WORD OF THE PROFESSOR if you're trying to select the best Soviet (Russian) team of all-time.

"For us, the best of times – a string of continuous successes – were the four seasons between 1981 and 1984," Igor Larionov wrote in his autobiography. "The time flew by as one happy moment. It seemed that this is how it would be forever."

The Russian team was an absolute force to be reckoned with during the early 1980s.

To be more specific, the Soviet team at the 1983 World Championship in West Germany topped all the great squads the country iced over the years. The Soviets went through the tournament winning nine of 10 games and outscoring the opposition 60-10, breezing to their 19th IIHF World Championship gold medal.

The Soviets' 1-1 tie with Czechoslovakia was played at a lightning tempo and described by many sportswriters as the greatest World Championship game of all-time. In spite of their impressive play, the Soviets finished tied with Czechoslovakia for first place in the medal round. But they were awarded the gold on the basis of a superior goals for/against differential – plus-10, to just plus-4 for Czechoslovakia.

The Soviet team was so dominant, it secured all six spots on the all-star team, with Vladislav Tretiak in goal, Slava Fetisov and Alexei Kasatonov on defense and Vladimir Krutov, Sergei Makarov and Larionov on the forward line.

Makarov led the tournament in scoring with nine goals and 18 points in just 10 games. Krutov was second with eight goals and 15 points.

Dave King, who coached the Canadian team, had told his players to slow the game down and control the tempo.

But although they had 19 NHLers in their lineup – including Marcel Dionne and Michel Goulet, two 50-plus goal-scorers – the Soviets toyed with them, trouncing the Canucks twice by the same score of 8-2.

Dionne, Charlie Simmer and Dave Taylor formed the Triple Crown Line – the highest scoring unit in the league – for the Los Angeles Kings. Goulet had scored 57 goals for Quebec, Dionne 56 for the Kings and Darryl Sittler 43 for Philadelphia.

"The Soviet teams of 1981-1984 era were so damn good they made us change the way the game is played," King said. "We were all still trying to play a forechecking game against them. We could do it for about 10 minutes, then they'd break it with a long pass and score.

"After that, teams started to lay back and play the 1-2-2, 1-3-1 or 1-4. That's where all the traps in hockey came from."

The only consolation for Canadians was that, through a strange quirk of fate, the World Championship trophy remained in Canada.

Bill Warwick, a member of the Penticton Vees who beat the Soviets to win the gold medal in 1955, had kept it all these years.

Warwick recalled that the trophy was falling apart when IIHF president Bunny Ahearne presented it to him in Krefeld, Germany.

He had a replica made and sent it back the next year with the Kitchener-Waterloo Dutchmen, who represented Canada in a tournament at Cortina d'Ampezzo, Italy that was held jointly as an Olympics and World Championship.

When the Russians struck gold in that tournament, Warwick had the last laugh.

"I saw the Russians skating around, holding up my phony trophy," he said. "I knew they had fallen for it."

CZECH REPUBLIC/CZECHOSLOVAKIA

1976 CANADA CUP

UNTIL SEPTEMBER OF 1976, the Soviet Union held the distinction of being the only nation to defeat a collection of Canada's best NHL players.

Team Czechoslovakia managed to shut down Bobby Orr and the rest of the Canadians for a 1–0 victory in the preliminary round of the 1976 Canada Cup.

But with 17,376 pro-Canadian supporters looking on at the Montreal Forum, Czechoslovakia broadened the base of top-level national sides by shutting out Team Canada 1-0 in the preliminary round of the inaugural Canada Cup tournament.

That's the main reason the 1976 Czechoslovakian team – and not the Dominik Hasek-led 1998 Olympic gold medal squad – is the best the country ever has iced.

"Yes, it must rank as the biggest victory in Czechoslovak hockey history," coach Jan Starsi told The Globe and Mail at the time.

"This is the finest Canadian team ever assembled. We showed that we could play excellent hockey, too, to win in this church of hockey, the Forum."

AN OUTBREAK OF INFLUENZA HIT THE CZECHOSLOVAK TEAM DURING THE TOURNAMENT, LEAVING IT WITH ONLY 12 PLAYERS ON THE BENCH IN A 7-1 CAKEWALK OVER POLAND AND SEVERELY WEAKENED FOR THE GOLD MEDAL SHOWDOWN WITH THE SOVIETS.

At the time, Jiri Holecek was considered the best goalie in Europe, having beaten the Soviet Union at the 1972 World Championship in Prague. However, Starsi decided to play 34-year-old Vladimir Dzurilla against Canada.

Dzurilla, a roly-poly puck-stopper who included beer as part of his training regimen, held Canadian sharpshooters Bobby Hull, Guy Lafleur, Phil Esposito and Bobby Orr off the scoresheet for 60 minutes and Milan Novy, later to play for the Washington Capitals, beat Rogie Vachon in the third period for the only goal of the game.

Canadian fans sat in stunned silence when the final siren sounded.

The two countries met again in a best-of-three series for the tournament title. And while Canada easily won the first game 6-0, it took an overtime marker by Darryl Sittler to clinch the championship for Canada with a 5-4 win in the second.

Most of the same Czechoslovak players had come within a single goal of scoring the first Olympics-World Championship double in the spring of that year. Playing for the gold medal at the 1976 Games in Innsbruck, Austria, Czechoslovakia led 3-2 and was only eight minutes away from a gold medal when Alexander Yakushev and Valery Kharlamov scored to give the Soviets a 4-3 victory, leaving their archrivals with the silver.

An outbreak of influenza hit the Czechoslovak team during the tournament, leaving it with only 12 players on the bench in a 7-1 cakewalk over Poland and severely weakened for the gold medal showdown with the Soviets.

Two months later, in Poland, the Czechoslovaks posted a 9-0-1 record, breezing to the World Championship gold. They outscored the opposition by a total of 67-14 while recording a win and a tie against the defending champion Soviets.

Although the gold was somewhat tainted because Canada did not compete, the U.S. team was stronger than usual because it used some NHL players for the first time after the International Ice Hockey Federation had lifted the ban on pro players.

"YES, IT MUST RANK AS THE BIGGEST VICTORY IN CZECHOSLOVAK HOCKEY HISTORY. THIS IS THE FINEST CANADIAN TEAM EVER ASSEMBLED. WE SHOWED THAT WE COULD PLAY EXCELLENT HOCKEY, TOO, TO WIN IN THIS CHURCH OF HOCKEY, THE FORUM."

– CZECHOSLOVAKIAN COACH JAN STARSI

Four of the six members of the all-star team – Holececk, defenseman Frantisek Pospisil, center Novy and winger Vladimir Martinec were from Czechoslovakia.

Peter Stastny, then a promising 19-year-old center who eventually defected in the summer of 1980, became the greatest NHL player the country ever produced and was inducted into the Hockey Hall of Fame.

Novy, left winger Jaroslav Pouzar, center Ivan Hlinka and defensemen Jiri Bubla and Miroslav Dvorak later were given permission by the Communist government to sign with NHL clubs in recognition of the faithful service for the national team. Pouzar earned Stanley Cup rings with the Edmonton Oilers in 1984 and 1985.

SWEDEN

2006 OLYMPICS

AFTER A PAIR FIFTH-PLACE FINISHES in the first two Olympic tournaments that included NHL players, Sweden entered the 2006 Olympic Winter Games in Turin, Italy, with something to prove. With veterans Peter Forsberg, Mats Sundin and Nicklas Lidstrom leading the way and upcoming talent in Henrik Zetterberg and the Sedin twins, the Swedes felt they had the perfect combination to challenge for Olympic gold. What resulted was the greatest performance in Swedish hockey history.

The Tre Kroner's confidence carried into the team's opening game against Kazakhstan, as they rolled to a 7-2 victory. However, the team was quickly brought back to Earth, falling 5-0 to a strong Russian team the following game. Sweden bounced back two days later with a 6-1 victory over Latvia, before beating the USA 2-1 just more than 24 hours later. The preliminary round, however, ended on a sour note, as the high-powered Swedes were shutout for the second time in four games, losing 3-0 to the undefeated Slovaks.

Heading into the elimination rounds of the tournament, the team's confidence was starting to build and the performance

The Tre Kroner's victory in 2006 was made even sweeter by the defeat of their rivals, Finland, in the final.

and leadership from the veterans was really starting to rub off on the younger players around them.

"We had guys on the team who were big stars," said Henrik Sedin. "Guys like Forsberg and Sundin had played in other Olympics and World Championships and we all learned a lot from them. People tend to build up these games much bigger than they are, but they are just regular hockey games and those guys really helped us realize that."

Sweden's mediocre 3-2 preliminary round record earned the team a quarterfinal date with Switzerland, who had only one loss in its opening five games. After a tight first period that the Swedes came out of with a 2-1 lead, they exploded in the second scoring three goals, two from the stick of Sundin. The two teams traded goals in the third period and the Swedes were off to the semifinals after a 6-2 victory.

> ## "BUT LOOKING BACK ONCE I'M RETIRED, WINNING THE OLYMPICS WILL DEFINITELY BE UP THERE AS ONE OF THE TOP MOMENTS OF MY CAREER.
>
> – HENRIK LUNDQVIST

The semis possessed an even greater challenge, with Sweden facing off against the Czech Republic, who knocked off the previously undefeated Slovaks. The Swedes remained poised and shocked the eventual bronze medal-winners with a big 7-3 win, setting up a gold medal match against their Scandinavian rivals from Finland, who had shutout Russia 4-0 to earn its berth in the final.

"Playing Finland was special, maybe not as much for us players, but for our fans and for our entire country," Sedin said. "Even in a World Championship game or a pre-tournament game, our fans always get really excited and playing them in the final was something extra special for our fans."

In the gold medal game, Finland opened the scoring on a power play goal by Kimmo Timonen at 14:45 of the first period. In the second, Zetterberg answered with a power play marker of his own and eight minutes later fellow Detroit Red Wing Niklas Kronwall put the Swedes up 2-1.

However, just a minute-and-a-half later the Finns tied it up when Ville Peltonen netted his fourth goal of the tournament. A mere

10 seconds into the third period a third Red Wing found the scoresheet for Sweden when Nicklas Lidstrom put them ahead for good. Swedish goaltender Henrik Lundqvist stopped all 10 shots he faced in the final frame, giving Sweden its second gold medal in 12 years and first with NHL competitors.

"I've had a couple of championships back home and obviously they meant a lot," Lundqvist said. "But looking back once I'm retired, winning the Olympics will definitely be up there as one of the top moments of my career."

FINLAND

2006 OLYMPICS

THE RESONATING QUOTE by Gaius Cassius Longinus also applies to Team Finland at the 2006 Turin Olympics. As the leading instigator in the plot to kill Julius Caesar 2,000 years ago, Cassius later died in a follow-up battle.

Goalie Antero Niittymaki took MVP honors in the 2006 Games after posting three shutouts in six games.

"In great attempts," Cassius said on his way down, "it is glorious even to fail."

So it is with the greatest Finnish team ever assembled. The Finns were rated the No. 6 nation by The Hockey News going into the 2006 Games. They won all fives games of their round robin by a combined score of 19-2, beat the Americans 4-3 in the quarterfinal, blanked the Russians 4-0 in the semifinal, then in the gold-medal game versus Sweden, well, Cassius said it best.

Or at least former NHLer Christian Ruutu did: "The most solid performance from the Finns came in Turin, but I think the loss in the final against 'the dear enemies' Swedes must have been the most bitter one as well."

"THE MOST SOLID PERFORMANCE FROM THE FINNS CAME IN TURIN, BUT I THINK THE LOSS IN THE FINAL AGAINST 'THE DEAR ENEMIES' SWEDES MUST HAVE BEEN THE MOST BITTER ONE AS WELL."

– CHRISTIAN RUUTU

In determining the best Team Finland ever, THN canvassed 10 Finnish pro scouts. Half of them selected the team that didn't win gold, but had a glorious run en route to a silver.

"It has to be the 2006 for three reasons," said Boston scout Jukka Holtari. "First, level of play. All the NHL players had a chance to play. Second, only the 3-2 loss to Sweden in eight games. Finland beat the Czech Republic, Canada, USA and Russia. Third, this was the last tournament where the first 'true professionals' generation of Finns were still together and making a real impact, players like Teemu Selanne, Saku Koivu, Ville Peltonen, Jere Lehtinen and Teppo Numminen."

Going into Turin, the defending Olympic champion Canadians were the top seed, followed by Czech Republic, Sweden, Russia and the United States in the top five. Finland and Slovakia weren't projected to make the semifinals. Finnish victories of 4-2 over the Czechs and 2-0 over Canada (plus wins over Switzerland, Germany and Italy) in the round robin opened eyes going into the medal round.

Calgary goalie Miikka Kiprusoff opted out of the tournament to rest a sore hip. Kiprusoff took the 2004 Finns to the World Cup final, so his absence was deemed critical. Without the Flames stopper, goaltending was left in the hands of Philadelphia Flyers rookie Antero Niittymaki.

But what the critics didn't take note of was 18 players returning from the World Cup team, including all seven defensemen – Sami Salo, Teppo Numminen, Kimmo Timonen, Toni Lydman, Aki Berg, Petteri Nummelin and Antti-Jussi Niemi.

Finland's forwards were a who's who of Suomi hockey. Teemu Selanne led the tournament with six goals and 11 points. Saku Koivu, Ville Peltonen, Olli Jokinen and Jere Lehtinen were all in the top eight in scoring.

"That team was the last real chance for the long-time core players to win something big together," said Montreal scout Hannu Laine. "Niittymaki proved to be a great goalie at high level. The team played entertaining hockey; the big names like Selanne and Koivu were on top of their national team careers and the young group led by Mikko Koivu and Tuomo Ruutu already had the experience and provided some leadership.

"It was also the last time Numminen played for Finland and it was really emotional for him. Losing to Sweden in the final game was hard for them and I think that was the closest Finland has come to winning a title when all the best players of the world were playing."

Finland has only won one major international event, but its 1995 world championship title is sullied because no NHLers were in that tournament due to the NHL lockout. "Yet that victory and that team probably had the strongest influence to Finnish hockey, hockey fans and Finnish people," said Tampa Bay scout Kari Kettunen.

Other Finnish teams receiving consideration as best ever from our panel of scouts were the 1991 Canada Cup team (third place), the 1994 world championship team (silver) and the 2004 World Cup team (runner-up to Canada).

"It has to be the silver medal team from Turin," said European Sport Services scout Janne Vuorinen. "Great team and great result."

SLOVAKIA

2002 WORLD CHAMPIONSHIP

Zigmund Palffy finished the 2002 World Championship with seven points in three games.

WHEN CZECHOSLOVAKIA split in 1993, hockey observers questioned the level of success the small nation of Slovakia could have.

Less than 10 years later, those questions were answered and punctuated with an exclamation mark when the country captured gold at the 2002 World Championship in Sweden, icing the greatest team in Slovakian history.

Led by players in their prime such as Zigmund Palffy, Lubomir Visnovsky and Michal Handzus, and long-time NHLers Jozef Stumpel and Peter Bondra, the Slovaks entered the tournament as significant underdogs. Slovakia had finished 13th in the 2002 Salt Lake City Winter Olympics just a few months prior and it was clear the team was looking to erase that memory.

"We were very mad at our team after finishing near last place at the Olympics," Visnovsky recalled. "We said we would come back to the World Championship and show everyone that the Slovakian hockey team could play much better."

Playing out of Group B, the Slovaks opened the tournament with wins against the Ukraine and Poland before falling to group winner Finland.

In the qualification round, the Slovaks impressed everyone by taking four of five games, posting victories over Ukraine, Sweden, Austria and Russia, but were again defeated by the Finns. Their 6-2 record earned them a quarterfinal date with the 7-1 Canadians.

"It was a very tough game," Visnovsky said. "We were down 2-0 and we ended up winning 3-2. It was a very important game for us."

The shocking win over Canada led to a semifinal showdown against the Swedes, who the Slovaks defeated 2-1 in the qualification round. The game was even tighter than the first, with the Slovaks erasing another 2-0 deficit to force the game into overtime and eventually a shootout. Slovakia won the shootout 1-0, earning the country's second trip to the World Championship final.

In the final, it was a rematch against the Russians, who the Slovaks toppled 6-4 in qualification. While Slovakia jumped out to an early lead in the first period, the game was far from over.

"We had such a great start to the game, I remember I scored in the first 20 seconds," Visnovsky said. "We dominated the first period, but by the third everything had changed and with about 10 minutes left the score was 3-3.

"Russia had very good offense and our team was starting to tire, so things didn't look great for us. Our first line of Palffy, Stumpel and Bondra had played a great game and Bondra scored the gold-winning goal with about two minutes remaining."

While a gold medal victory is impressive in itself, defeating squads as strong as Canada, Sweden and Russia along the way made the victory even more special to the players involved.

"When you beat top teams, especially when we were down 2-0 to both Canada and Sweden, it shows we had a good team and our victory wasn't a fluke," Handzus said. "We went through the tournament...beating all the best teams, including Sweden twice on their home ice."

The gold medal was Slovakia's first since the dissolution of Czechoslovakia and remains the only gold won by a Slovakian hockey team.

And although the 2010 Slovakian Olympic hockey team's fourth-place finish in Vancouver impressed many, 2002 is the year the players will always remember.

"For a European player, the World Championship is like the NHL's Stanley Cup," Visnovsky said. "The gold medal was so big for Slovakian hockey and for all of Slovakia. I came back from Sweden and everyone was waiting for us on the streets. Everyone was so excited…it was a great feeling for me and my teammates."

Visnovsky was not alone in his assessment of what the '02 gold meant.

"In Slovakia, they don't have a lot of coverage of the NHL, so we grow up following the national team and we dream of playing at the World Championship," Handzus said. "The Stanley Cup is a big prize, but for us to win gold at the World Championship, it was huge for us and our country."

WORLD JUNIOR CHAMPIONSHIP

2005

Patrice Bergeron, Sidney Crosby and Corey Perry were only a handful of the future stars Canada had at its disposal for the 2005 world juniors.

If there was one good thing that came out of the NHL work stoppage in 2004-05, it was the quality of players available to countries at the World Junior Championship.

The gold-medal Canadians were brimming with NHL-calibre talent. Center Patrice Bergeron had spent the previous season in the NHL with Boston and had 39 points as an 18-year-old. He was the scoring leader (five goals and 13 points in six games) as Canada won gold at the 2005 WJC in Grand Forks, N.D.

The Canadians also had at least two or more players who surely would have made the NHL as 19-year-olds in 2004-05 and not been at the 2005 WJC. Consider these names: Ryan Getzlaf, Jeff Carter, Corey Perry, Dion Phaneuf and Mike Richards. They all remained in major junior while the NHL and the players' association negotiated a new collective bargaining agreement. But it wasn't just the lockout that boosted the talent at the WJC.

"Take a look at the 2003 draft," one scout offered. "That draft will probably go down as the best one after the 1979 draft. The players drafted in 2003 were 19, going on 20 at the 2005 world juniors. And there were a ton of excellent Canadians in that 2003 draft."

The other Team Canada members drafted in 2003 were Brent Seabrook, Shea Weber, Braydon Coburn, Nigel Dawes, Colin Fraser, Clarke MacArthur, Anthony Stewart, Shawn Belle, Stephen Dixon, Jeremy Colliton and Rejean Beauchemin.

If that's not already a recipe for the best WJC team ever, Canada also had 17-year-old Sidney Crosby, who went on to be the first overall NHL draft pick in 2005. Crosby had six goals and nine points in six games. Also on the roster were early 2004 draft picks Cam Barker and Andrew Ladd.

Canada outscored the opposition 32-5 in the four round robin games, then beat the Czech Republic 3-1 in the semifinal and Russia 6-1 in the gold-medal game.

All but Dixon and goalies Jeff Glass and Beauchemin have gone on to play in the NHL.

"The NHL star power is the tipping point for this team in my opinion," said THN senior writer Ken Campbell, who has covered seven world juniors. "But I don't think you can totally discount the 1995 team. There certainly wasn't the star power on that team that there was in 2005, but almost every player on that team went on to have at least a solid NHL career.

"I believe the 1995 edition was the first Canadian team to go 7-0-0 in the tournament and it did so against much more difficult competition. The tournament was smaller and it was a round-robin event in which each game meant something and, unlike the 2005 team, the Canadians were playing against a united USSR and Czechoslovakia."

"THE 2003 DRAFT WILL PROBABLY GO DOWN AS THE BEST ONE AFTER THE 1979 DRAFT. THE PLAYERS DRAFTED IN 2003 WERE 19, GOING ON 20 AT THE 2005 WORLD JUNIORS. AND THERE WERE A TON OF EXCELLENT CANADIANS IN THAT 2003 DRAFT."

– AN NHL SCOUT

Canada's team at the 1995 WJC had four players named to the all-star team – Bryan McCabe, Jason Allison, Marty Murray and Eric Daze – a first and only for any nation. The 2005 team placed Phaneuf, Bergeron and Carter on the all-star team. McCabe was the best defenseman and Murray the best forward at the 1995 tournament, while Phaneuf was best defenseman in 2005.

Jeff O'Neill, who was on that 1995 edition, once came up with this, when comparing the 2005 team to the 1995 team: "We played against stiff competition and they played against stiffs."

That's not true, says one scout.

"The other teams in the 2005 tournament had players such as Ovechkin, Malkin, Kessel, etc., so they were not too shabby, either."

Said Detroit assistant GM Jim Nill: "Our Olympic team (in 2010) and for the next 10 years will be anchored by members on (the 2005 Canadian) team."

Also getting consideration on the short list was the 1989 Soviet Union team that had the tournament's top line of Sergei Fedorov, Alexander Mogilny and Pavel Bure. That team swept the competition and outscored its foes 48-10.

WOMEN'S

2010 OLYMPICS

IT MIGHT SEEM HASTY TO SUGGEST the Canadian Women's team that won gold at the 2010 Olympics is the best collection of female players ever, but when you examine how it won and the depth of skill it leaned on, it's fitting to hang them with the No. 1 label.

In Vancouver, the 2010 Canadian team proved it could throttle you with offense – including an 18-0 steamrolling of Slovakia and 13-1 walloping of Sweden – just as easily as it could play the kind of controlled defensive game that beat their arch-rivals from America in the tournament's final game.

The Canadian team came together like no other and dominated the competition at the 2010 Games in Vancouver.

But the Swedes should consider themselves fortunate to have scored at all on the Canadians. Only one other team (Switzerland) could manage to score a single goal – and both goals Canada allowed came in the preliminary round.

Team Canada's skill was matched only by its depth: Shannon Szabados, the 23-year-old netminder who won Canada's final game, was named best goalie of the Games, but coach Melody Davidson could've just as easily given the nod to veterans Kim St-Pierre or Charline Labonte, who had been instrumental in past Canadian gold medal wins.

And if observers could see diminishing roles for some veteran Canadian players, it wasn't due to a fall-off in their play; rather, it was because the monster known as Meghan Agosta (the tournament's top scorer and most valuable player) and 19-year-old phenom Marie-Philip Poulin were making them share the spotlight.

"THE COMPETITION IS TOUGHER NOW TO MAKE THE TEAM, THE PREPARATION IS GREATER AND WE HAD MORE TIME TO BE TOGETHER, SO THE PERFORMANCES ARE BETTER."

– HAYLEY WICKENHEISER

It took a veteran such as Hayley Wickenheiser, Canada's captain and someone who has skated in every Olympics since female players began participating in 1998, to put the Canadian 2010 team in perspective.

"The best team of all-time I think was this year's team, in terms of top-to-bottom quality, overall skill level, fitness level and execution," Wickenheiser said. "I don't know that we had our strongest 'D' corps I've ever seen, but as a team, as an overall unit, this one was best.

"The competition is tougher now to make the team, the preparation is greater and we had more time to be together, so the performances are better."

Prior to the Vancouver Games, Team USA cornerstone Angela Ruggiero spoke of the respect she held for the program Canada has put together for its female players.

"You can't argue with success and two straight gold medals for (Canada) means you have to give them their due," Ruggiero said in the fall of 2008, before the Canadians extended their Olympic run to three consecutive gold medal victories. "Don't get me wrong, I believe in (the U.S.) program. But the time and effort that Canada invests in its female players is really great for the sport and it shows in the results that they've gotten up to this point."

And after Canada's domination in Vancouver with a team for the ages, one might assume those results are going to continue.

NHL TEAMS

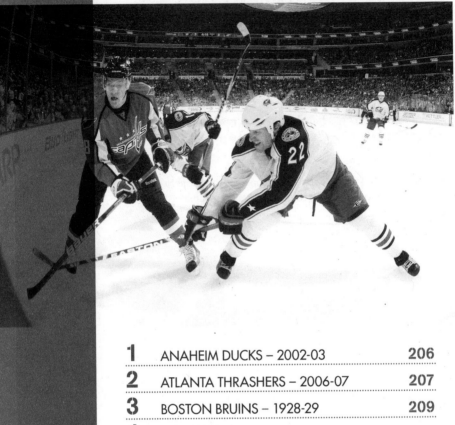

1 ANAHEIM DUCKS – 2002-03

Despite losing in seven games in the 2003 Cup final, Mighty Ducks goalie Jean-Sebastien Giguere took home the Conn Smythe Trophy as playoff MVP after going 15–6 with a 1.62 GAA and .945 SP.

AT A TIME when they were still the Mighty Ducks of Anaheim, an underdog group of mostly unknowns came within a whisker of hoisting the Stanley Cup.

Thanks to stout defensive play and the incredible goaltending of Conn Smythe Trophy winner Jean-Sebastien Giguere, the 2002-03 Mighty Ducks slayed the best teams in the West en route to a date in the final with the New Jersey Devils.

"I don't think anybody would have thought we had that at the beginning of the year," Giguere said of the run. "What we had was a young, hardworking team; a team that was well coached. We played very well defensively and it seemed like everybody was helping out and doing their job very well."

With rookie bench boss Mike Babcock at the helm, the Mighty Ducks were the most unlikely of Western Conference champs. The seventh seed heading into the post-season, the Ducks nevertheless pulled off a stunning first round upset over the powerhouse Detroit Red Wings, who won the Cup the year before.

And though name recognition in Anaheim was limited to Paul Kariya and Adam Oates, the workmanlike squad quickly realized the field was wide open, especially with fellow upstart Minnesota upsetting Colorado and Vancouver along the way.

"When we got to the playoffs, we had nothing to lose," Giguere recalled. "We went in there trying to have a good experience and trying to have fun and you never know when you start getting hot where that can lead you.

"Obviously we beat Detroit in the first round…still, there was a long road ahead of us. We beat Dallas in six and I think that was a big challenge for us. What we saw was Minnesota getting really tired playing against Vancouver – they went all the way to Game 7 – and we felt we had an advantage going into that series. We wanted to take advantage, which we did."

Defensively savvy players such as Sammy Pahlsson and Rob Niedermayer were key to the run, though the Devils were the masters of defensive hockey and put an end to Anaheim's Cinderella run in Game 7 of the Stanley Cup final.

"Obviously we beat Detroit in the first round…still, there was a long road ahead of us. We beat Dallas in six and I think that was a big challenge for us. What we saw was Minnesota getting really tired playing against Vancouver – they went all the way to Game 7 – and we felt we had an advantage going into that series. We wanted to take advantage, which we did."

Defensively savvy players such as Sammy Pahlsson and Rob Niedermayer were key to the run, though the Devils were the masters of defensive hockey and put an end to Anaheim's Cinderella run in Game 7 of the Stanley Cup final.

2 ATLANTA THRASHERS – 2006-07

CONSIDERING THE HISTORY of the Atlanta Thrashers – winners of zero post-season games in a decade of existence – the concept of "best team" is, to say the least, somewhat relative.

Although the New York Rangers swept them in the first round, the 2006-07 Thrashers won a Southeast Division title and made the playoffs. Those are two accomplishments no other Atlanta team can claim, which is why they're THN's choice as top team in the organization's history.

The '06-07 Thrashers took a hit before the season, when high-scoring center Marc Savard left for Boston in the summer. However, you wouldn't have known by their record; they started the year with an 8-2-3 mark through the month of October and benefited from solid goaltending by Kari Lehtonen and a veteran-heavy collection (including Slava Kozlov, Scott Mellanby and

Bobby Holik), whose experience was valued by coach Bob Hartley and GM Don Waddell.

"Lehtonen was probably the best goalie in the league for the first two months of that year and that's what got them off to a good start," said former NHL goalie and TV analyst Darren Eliott, who has covered all Thrashers games since the team's inception in 1999.

Still, there's no doubt there were two straws stirring the drink for that Atlanta team: franchise cornerstone Ilya Kovalchuk and linemate Marian Hossa. Kovalchuk potted 42 goals while Hossa became the first Atlanta player to post 100 points.

Wanting to capitalize on the team's new-found success, Waddell added two veterans – left winger Keith Tkachuk and defenseman Alexei Zhitnik – at the trade deadline.

Unfortunately, no Thrasher did much of anything come the postseason. Atlanta scored just five times on Rangers goalie Henrik Lundqvist and bowed out meekly in four games.

"A lot of things unraveled for them very quickly once they made the playoffs," Eliott said. "That might be the best team the organization has had, but looking back it still seems like it was built like a house of cards."

Ilya Kovalchuk helped get the Thrashers into the playoffs in 2006–07, but couldn't find a victory against the Rangers.

3 BOSTON BRUINS – 1928-29

THE NHL WAS STILL TRYING to figure itself out in the 1920s (the New York Americans were the only American team in the Canadian Division, for example), but by decade's end, the Boston Bruins reached an iron-clad conclusion: If the other team can't score, it can't win.

Enter Cecil 'Tiny' Thompson, who joined the Bruins just in time for them to move into Boston Garden and christen it with the franchise's first Stanley Cup in 1929.

Playing behind an early version of a shutdown defense pair – Hall of Famer Eddie Shore and captain Lionel Hitchman – Thompson began a 10-year run between Boston's pipes by posting a 1.15 regular season goals-against average, then nearly halved that during the playoffs.

Defenseman Eddie Shore won the Hart Trophy as NHL MVP four times during his 15-year NHL career.

Thompson's post-season GAA over a five-game playoff sweep (3-0 against the Montreal Canadiens; 2-0 over the New York Rangers in the league's first all-American Cup final) was 0.60, with three shutouts. But at 5-foot-10 and 160-pounds, 'Tiny' was hardly diminutive, so what's with the nickname?

"We've investigated that and we don't even know," said Kevin Shea, the Hockey Hall of Fame's editor of publications and on-line features. "It was a childhood thing, whether he was the runt of the family or whether it was a teasing thing with the kids in the neighborhood. He didn't seem to be particularly short in that era...It wasn't like Roy Worters or one of those guys who was 5-foot-2."

Under Cy Denneny, spending his only season in Boston as player-coach, the Bruins started slowly (they even lost their first game at the Garden), but eventually reeled off a then NHL-record 13-game unbeaten streak (11-0-2), not losing for the entire month of January.

Denneny had enough offense to support all that defense and goaltending, because GM Art Ross built a team two lines deep. Bruins scoring leader Harry Oliver (17 goals, 23 points) played on one line, while the Dynamite Line – Dutch Gainor (14 goals), Cooney Weiland (11) and Dit Clapper (nine) netted their fair share as well (Shore also potted 12). That trio scored five of the nine goals the B's needed to sweep five playoff games.

4 BUFFALO SABRES – 1974-75

Rene Robert, who had his one and only 100-point season in 1974–75, was one-third of the Sabres famed French Connection line, along with Gilbert Perreault and Rick Martin.

NOT ONLY WAS 1974-75 a breakout season for the Buffalo Sabres, it was also a coming out party for the famed 'French Connection' line.

Led by the trio of Rene Robert, Gilbert Perreault and Rick Martin, who combined for 291 regular season points (89 more points than the season prior), the Sabres won 49 games. In the semifinals, Buffalo bested the juggernaut Canadiens – who began a run of four-straight Stanley Cups the next year – and advanced to the final for the first time in franchise history.

Up against the Philadelphia Flyers, the Sabres lost the first two games on the road and entered a virtual must-win situation at home in Game 3.

But the 'Broad Street Bullies' weren't the only obstacle the Sabres had to overcome to secure a victory; due to unusually hot weather in Buffalo, thick fog covered the ice for large portions of the contest – the soup made it tough for players to see much of anything on the ice.

"Every three or four minutes we'd have to go out and skate around with towels to try and get the fog off," Martin said.

Nevertheless the game continued and in overtime the 'French Connection' connected. Taking a pass from Perreault in the Flyers zone, Robert fired a shot through goaltender Bernie Parent's legs giving the Sabres a 5-4 victory.

But the celebrations were short lived; Buffalo lost two of the next three games, giving Philadelphia their second straight Stanley Cup.

"It was great to get there, but there has to be a winner and a loser and unfortunately we were the loser," Martin said. "So that's a bit of a downer."

It took the Sabres 24 years to return to the final and the franchise is still looking for its first Stanley Cup, but that 1974-75 team was something special.

5 CALGARY FLAMES – 1985-86

YOU COULD CALL THE 1985-86 Calgary Flames 'great' by the simple fact they broke up perhaps the greatest dynasty in the history of hockey. The powerhouse Edmonton Oilers won Stanley Cups in 1984, '85, '87, '88 and '90. An upset loss to Calgary in 1986 broke up what could have been a run of five straight Cups and six in seven years. "After we beat the Oilers, we thought 'this is the year,' " said former Flames great Lanny McDonald. "Chances like that, especially after beating Edmonton, don't happen often." The 1985-86 Flames were an offensive powerhouse built around the marksmanship of leading scorer Joe Mullen (acquired from St. Louis) and Hakan Loob, the playmaking of Dan Quinn, the veteran leadership of McDonald, John Tonelli and Doug Risebrough, the mobile defense of Al MacInnis and Gary Suter and the clutch goaltending of Mike Vernon.

Calgary finished sixth overall during the regular season, 30 points behind the top-seeded Oilers. In Game 7 of the division final against Edmonton, the teams were tied 2-2 going into the third period before the 'gaffe of the century.'

Lanny McDonald helped the Calgary Flames upset the dynastic Oilers, but couldn't get past the Canadiens in the final.

Oilers defenseman Steve Smith attempted a 100-foot pass from behind his own net at the 5:14 mark. It hit goalie Grant Fuhr's pad and caromed into Edmonton's net to put the Flames up 3-2. Smith fell to the ice with head in hands and was in tears later.

Calgary needed seven games to beat St. Louis in the conference final, then faced the upstart Montreal Canadiens, with rookie goalie Patrick Roy, in the Cup final. The Flames won the opener 5-2, but blew a 2-0 lead in Game 2 and lost on Brian Skrudland's winner nine seconds into overtime. The Habs won the series 4-1.

"After losing in '86, you automatically believe you're going right back again next year," McDonald said. "We were so damn talented across the board. But it took us three more years to get back in '89."

6 CAROLINA HURRICANES – 2005-06

FEW WOULD ARGUE losing a year of hockey over a labor dispute was a good thing, but it sure helped the Carolina Hurricanes.

When play resumed after the 2004-05 lockout, the 'New NHL' was born and no team transitioned better or faster than the Hurricanes. Coach Peter Laviolette believed the NHL would be steadfast this time after many failed crackdowns on obstruction and preached discipline with his team, penalizing them with extra laps at practice any time a soft hook was used in place of hard stride.

"Early on, I think we had the best grasp of any team on the rules," captain Rod Brind'Amour said midway through the 2005-06 season. "Right from Day 1 at training camp, before we ever stepped on the ice, we had a meeting and (Laviolette) said there would be consequences for hooking, holding and interference. The point was driven home that these things would not be allowed moving forward."

The other ramification of the lockout was it forced Eric Staal into a year of American League hockey. Staal had a modest 31-point season as a 20-year-old rookie in 2003-04, but after a year of minor league seasoning, he became an NHL star as a sophomore, leading the Canes with 45 goals and 100 points.

Carolina's other young hero didn't emerge until the second game of the playoffs when a 22-year-old Cam Ward replaced Martin Gerber in goal. The Canes had already lost Game 1 of their first round series with Montreal and dropped Game 2 in overtime, falling behind 2-0 with two home-ice losses.

But after being exposed to playoff hockey in the extra-time setback, Ward started Game 3 and won his next seven outings. Carolina eliminated Montreal and New Jersey, then won seven-game series over Buffalo and Edmonton to claim its first Cup in franchise history, with Ward becoming the first rookie goalie to win the Conn Smythe since Patrick Roy in 1986.

7 CHICAGO BLACKHAWKS – 1933-34

THE CHICAGO BLACK HAWKS quite literally experienced the early days of the Great Depression. They won just seven games in each of their 1927-28 and 1928-29 seasons.

Those were the first two seasons of goalie Charlie Gardiner's NHL career. Born in Edinburgh, Scotland and raised in Winnipeg, Gardiner was molded into the ultimate competitor those formative years. When he lost close games, he'd cry. When he was booed, he thought about quitting. When he stopped an opponent on a breakaway, he had the nerve to puff his chest and say, "Tough luck, try again some time."

Gardiner was also called the greatest goalkeeper in the world by many observers. Even the legendary Howie Morenz once said, "He was the hardest netman I ever tried to outguess."

In Gardiner's seven seasons, only three time did Chicago have a winning record and only four times make the playoffs. Yet, in that time, he won the Vezina twice and was a first-team all-star three times, while posting a career goals-against average of 1.43 in Stanley Cup play.

When the Black Hawks made it to the Cup final in 1934, the goaltender effectively sacrificed his life to win it all. Ignoring a painful tonsil infection that spread through his body that spring, Gardiner led Chicago to 2-1 and 4-1 victories in the first two games against Detroit.

The Wings bounced back for a 5-2 win in Game 3 and in the dressing room after the game, Gardiner and teammate Johnny Gottselig argued and got into a fight that had to be broken up by team owner Frederic McLaughlin.

Gardiner became ill during the night and had to be taken to hospital. Still, he insisted on playing in Game 4 at Chicago Stadium and it's a good thing he did. Gardiner and Detroit goalie Wilf Cude were unbeatable during 60 minutes of regulation time and it took 30 minutes of overtime before Chicago's Harold 'Mush' March scored the Cup winning goal.

As for the ailing Gardiner, he paid the ultimate price for playing in pain a few days later when he collapsed and was rushed to hospital. In a coma, he died June 13, 1934 at age 29 from a brain hemorrhage, originating from the tonsillar infection he'd earlier dismissed.

8 COLORADO AVALANCHE – 1995-96

FOR COLORADO, the first Cup was the deepest. And the sweetest.

Having arrived in Denver from Quebec City in the summer of 1995 with a roster brimming with young studs, the newly minted Avalanche was primed for greatness.

"When I took over '94-95 in Quebec, that team had the ingredients," said then Avalanche GM Pierre Lacroix.

Well, nearly all the ingredients. Nothing like "complementing" your roster with arguably the greatest goalie of all-time. In the midst of a three-game losing streak in December, Lacroix landed the disgruntled Montreal Canadiens stopper, along with forward Mike Keane, for Jocelyn Thibault, Martin Rucinsky and Andrei Kovalenko. It was a deal, and steal, for the ages.

Of course, Roy played behind stellar talent. The dynamic duo of centers Joe Sakic and Peter Forsberg finished third and fifth in league scoring as Colorado averaged nearly four goals per game in the regular season. Other key cogs included wingers

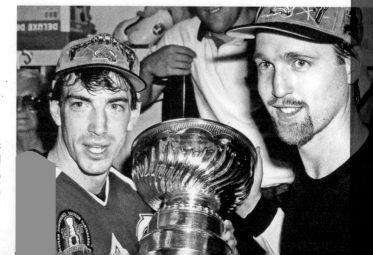

Joe Sakic and Patrick Roy were the focal points of the Avs 1996 Cup win, the first in franchise history.

Claude Lemieux, Valeri Kamensky and Adam Deadmarsh, and defensemen Sandis Ozolinsh and Sylvain Lefebvre.

The 1995-96 Avs finished third overall in the regular season with 104 points, but really started to click in the playoffs. They carved through the Western Conference in three series of six games, including a barn-burning conference final matchup with their new blood rivals from Detroit. Once they'd dispensed with the best in the west, the Avalanche met the Cinderella Florida Panthers in the final.

Taking the first two games at home by a combined 11-2 count, the Avs won Game 3 in Miami 3-2 and outlasted the Panthers in a triple-overtime Game 4 when defenseman Uwe Krupp connected with a point shot. Sakic won the Conn Smythe with 18 goals and 34 points in 22 games.

The win gave the city of Denver its first pro sports championship and began a love affair with the team and the sport.

"It was fun to see hockey develop there," Roy said, "especially in youth hockey because my sons were playing in Denver and the level of play was increasing year after year."

9 COLUMBUS BLUE JACKETS – 2008-09

NOTED AS A DEFENSIVE-MINDED COACH, Ken Hitchcock's game plan helped elevate Columbus to the playoffs for the first time in 2008-09, eight seasons into the franchise's existence.

But the backbone to any good team, defense-first or not, is a good goalie. And while 20-year-old Steve Mason garnered much attention by posting 10 shutouts and earning the Calder Trophy, 'Hitch' said he was impressed by how the youngster handled the increasing expectations.

"I thought he was immune to the pressure," Hitchcock said. "His ability to play the way he did really helped us sell to the rest of the players on the commitment necessary. Once we could see we could play and win one-goal games, the buy-in was pretty easy."

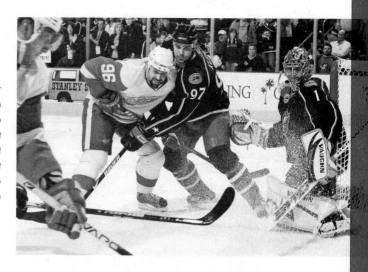

Steve Mason's Calder Trophy–winning season led the Blue Jackets into the playoffs for the first time, but he couldn't find his game against the Red Wings, who swept Columbus in the opening round.

The maturation of the team's captain and offensive catalyst as a two-way player was also important in Columbus' development. Rick Nash saw his plus-minus improve by nine, but he also put up his highest point-total in his career to that point and accumulated 40 goals for the second time.

But aside from the two stars, Hitchcock attributes much of the success to the team's defense corps, namely the top pairing of Jan Hejda and off-season free agent signing Mike Commodore.

"Hejda and Commodore gave us a pair that was able to check down the best players," Hitchcock said. "When we had players we knew could compete against the other team's top guys it became a lot easier for the coaching staff."

And, despite getting swept by the second-seeded Red Wings in the first round, qualifying for the playoffs for the first time went a long way in finally establishing Columbus as a legitimate NHL franchise.

"I think making the playoffs validates your team," Hitchcock explained. "Us making it in the playoffs was a relief to everybody in the city because it made us feel a part of the NHL."

10 DALLAS STARS – 1997-98

Ed Belfour's 1.88 GAA was the best in the NHL in his first season in Dallas.

THE 1997-98 SEASON was a bounce-back campaign for the Stars and laid the ground work for their Stanley Cup championship the following year.

After being upset in the previous playoffs by the Oilers, Dallas won their first and only Presidents' Trophy and advanced to the Western Conference final. Though they were defeated by the eventual Stanley Cup champion Detroit Red Wings in six games, it was a memorable season for both fans and players.

"I knew that we were doing something big when we would see and hear the home crowds during the regular season and the playoffs that year," said former Stars center and current GM Joe Nieuwendyk. "Looking back, the '98 playoff run was the start of a very good run for the Stars."

Leading the way was resurgent goaltender Ed Belfour, who signed with Dallas on July 2, 1997 before posting a career high 37 wins and putting up a league best 1.88 goals-against average. Belfour's regular season numbers only improved in the playoffs with a 1.79 GAA and a .922 save percentage.

It was a bounce-back year for Belfour as well as the team. His starting job in Chicago began to slip away during the '96 season, winning only 22 games in 50 appearances. The following season, after posting just 11 wins in 33 games, he was traded to San Jose. A 3-9-0 record, 3.41 GAA and .884 SP with the Sharks didn't earn Belfour a contract extension and forced him to free agency where the Stars signed him.

"He was unbelievable," Nieuwendyk said. "Belfour really found his groove and put up some impressive performances almost every night during the 1998 playoffs."

11 DETROIT RED WINGS – 1942-43

Unlike their former teammate Sid Abel, Johnny Mowers' and Syd Howe's names don't hang from the rafters at Joe Louis Arena in Detroit. In fact, the name Mowers may not even conjure up a response from the average hockey fan. But in 1942-43, along with Howe, Mowers played a major role in helping the Red Wings to their third Stanley Cup.

It was Mowers' third season as the Red Wings goaltender and he finished the regular season with a league-best 25 wins, six shutouts and a 2.47 goals-against average en route to a Vezina Trophy. Howe, who the Wings had purchased from the St. Louis Eagles nine years earlier, finished first among all Red Wings players with 55 points.

"He was certainly a great offensive player," said hockey historian Ernie Fitzsimmons of Howe. "He was a consistent scorer and that pickup they made, getting him from St. Louis was a pretty big deal."

In the playoffs, Mowers' outstanding numbers improved; he won eight of 10 games, posting a 1.94 GAA and two shutouts.

"He was certainly the dominant goalie that season," Fitzsimmons said. "Whether that was all his fault or not is hard to say. I think Detroit had several experienced players. A team like the New York Rangers had 12 rookies, Detroit had two."

After the '43 season Mowers enlisted in the Royal Canadian Air Force and served in the Second World War. He returned to the Red Wings only to retire from the NHL a year later. Howe, on the other hand, played two more seasons with the Wings and continued to be one of their prime offensive producers, tallying 49 goals and 113 points.

Although neither Mowers nor Howe will be mentioned in the same sentence as Detroit legends Gordie Howe, Ted Lindsay or Terry Sawchuk, both were important parts during an important era for one of the most successful NHL franchises of all-time.

12 EDMONTON OILERS – 1989-90

FIRST CAME THE WAYNE GRETZKY trade in the summer of 1988. Then came a Round 1 playoff upset at the hands of the Los Angeles Kings in the spring of 1989. There was no funeral, but there was a feeling of loss: the Edmonton Oilers dynasty was gone.

Or so went conventional wisdom.

An ominous first month saw the 1989-90 Oilers sitting below .500. Center Jimmy Carson, a major piece acquired for Gretzky, was moved to Detroit in early November for a package that included youngsters Adam Graves and Joe Murphy.

And the Oilers surged. By late-December they pieced together a nine-game unbeaten streak. While some of the faces of the old era led the team in scoring – Mark Messier, Jari Kurri, Glenn Anderson – it was the next generation of players that gave the team balance and depth.

"The Kid Line (Graves, Murphy and Martin Gelinas) was something John Muckler took a chance on because they were trying to insert a young guy on each line and there just wasn't that chemistry," said Bill Ranford, who emerged as the team's No. 1 goalie that season. "I think our team realized that when that line became a shutdown line we could have some success."

The Oilers finished second in the Smythe Division and drew the Winnipeg Jets in Round 1. After falling behind 3-1 in the series, Ranford started hearing it from Oilers supporters.

Finnish-born Esa Tikkanen was fourth in team scoring in the 1989–90 playoff with 24 points in 22 games.

"I took a lot of heat in the media over the way it started and I think that was probably my determination: to prove them wrong," said Ranford, the '90 Conn Smythe winner.

Edmonton mounted a comeback and won its next eight games to blow past Winnipeg and Los Angeles and get an early lead on the Chicago Blackhawks, who they beat 4-2. Edmonton disposed of the Bruins in five games, allowing only eight goals in the series and earning their fifth Cup in seven years.

And the dynasty wasn't quite dead after all.

13 FLORIDA PANTHERS – 1995-96

AFTER MISSING THE PLAYOFFS by a single point in each of the franchise's first two years of existence, the Year of the Rat proved to be a special one for the Florida Panthers.

The luck was foreshadowed at the beginning of the 1995-96 season at the team's home-opener when Scott Mellanby set off what would become the team's calling.

Shortly before they took the ice, a rat scurried into the dressing room and made a beeline for the Panthers' leading scorer that season.

"As it got to me, really out of self defense more than anything – and probably fear – I just one-timed it," Mellanby chuckled. "Probably the best one-timer of my career, because I certainly wasn't going to rival Brett Hull for one-timing the puck."

Mellanby scored two goals that night, which led goalie John Vanbiesbrouck to remark the right winger had achieved the 'rat trick.' It was a theme that began to pick up steam, culminating in a shower of plastic rats raining on the ice after each home goal.

The Panthers began the season with 14 wins in 18 games and didn't stumble until they wrapped up the year with a 6-12-2 stint, leaving them fourth in the conference. What followed was an unlikely run to the Stanley Cup final from a team of checkers who might have been considered spare parts on other teams.

Vanbiesbrouck was spectacular, posting a .932 save percentage and 2.25 goals-against average with a 12-10 record in his most successful playoffs.

After beating Boston, Philadelphia and Pittsburgh, however, the Panthers ran into a strong Colorado Avalanche squad that overwhelmed them. The Panthers lost 3-1, 8-1 and 3-2 in the first three games and forced Game 4 into the third overtime period, before Uwe Krupp put the Cinderella run to rest.

"It amazes me how well that team did, period," Mellanby said of his Panthers. "That team had a unique chemistry and I wish you could bottle it."

Goalie John Vanbiesbrouck's .932 SP and 2.25 GAA were a big reason for the Panthers' unexpected playoff run.

14 LOS ANGELES KINGS – 1992-93

After missing nearly half the regular season, Wayne Gretzky put up 40 points in just 24 playoff games while leading the Kings to the 1993 final.

THE 1992-93 SEASON was a rollercoaster ride for the Los Angeles Kings, but in the end finished as the greatest in franchise history.

The Kings were coming off a 10th overall finish and a first round exit in the playoffs the season prior. Rookie coach Barry Melrose planned to put the onus on some youngsters, guys in their early 20s with just a year or two of experience in the league, notably on the blueline.

"We might take some lumps early," Melrose said prior to that season.

Those knocks came earlier than expected when star center Wayne Gretzky was lost with a herniated disc in his back during training camp. At the time there was speculation Gretzky would have to retire and the Kings were just hoping he'd return at some point during the season.

Instead of folding the surprising Kings were on pace to set a team record for wins after 25 games. But the hockey gods are a fickle group and by the halfway mark L.A. had stumbled. Gretzky returned for Game 39, but Melrose was benching stars such as Jari Kurri; Paul Coffey was traded after scoring 57 points in 50 games; and Kelly Hrudey, the team's No. 1 netminder, fell into what he described as the worst slump of his career.

"We had to fight tooth-and-nail to resurrect my career," Hrudey said.

Los Angeles finished sixth in the Campbell Conference and was primed to lose early in the playoffs. But it didn't happen.

The Kings bested division rivals Calgary and Vancouver in Rounds 1 and 2, then went seven games with Toronto in the conference final, winning 5-4 on a Gretzky goal. The Kings moved on to face Patrick Roy and the Montreal Canadiens, losing the championship series 4-1, but making a name for themselves with their first, and only, trip to the Stanley Cup final.

15 MINNESOTA WILD – 2002-03

LITTLE WAS EXPECTED of the 2002-03 Minnesota Wild after their first two campaigns as an expansion outfit proved lackluster. But a record-setting post-season vaulted the franchise into relevancy and provided the team's best season.

Carried by a 20-year-old Marian Gaborik and a solid team game plan led by players like Pascal Dupuis and Andrew Brunette, as well as Jack Adams Award-winning coaching by Jacques Lemaire, Minnesota clinched its first playoff spot as the Wild after a 42-win regular season.

In the first round of the playoffs, the Wild found themselves down 3-1 to the Avalanche before rallying to win Game 5 on the road and Game 6 at home in overtime. Back in Denver for a do-or-die Game 7, the Wild knocked out the Avalanche 3:25 into overtime on a goal by the veteran Brunette.

"It was such a rewarding goal, not just for myself, but for the entire team," Brunette said.

In the West semifinal, the Wild again found themselves down 3-1, this time against the Canucks, heading for a Game 5 on enemy ice.

"This was different than the Colorado series, we felt we deserved to be up 3-1," Brunette said. "We had a lot of confidence

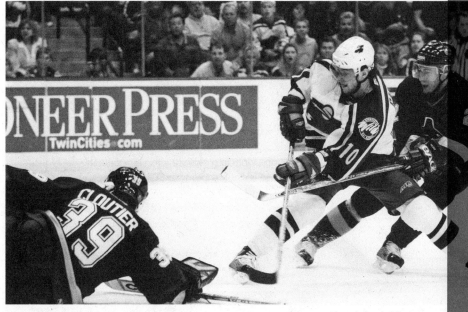

and liked the way we were playing and just wanted to keep it up."

That belief propelled the Wild to a dominating 7-2 win in Game 5 and they again came from behind to claim the series in seven games.

Although they were swept by Jean-Sebastien Giguere and the Mighty Ducks in the conference final – scoring just a single goal in the series – the Wild became the first and only team in NHL history to come back from two 3-1 deficits in a single post-season.

"We all accepted and cherished our roles that season," Brunette said. "We were all unselfish in the way we played.

"We just all wanted to be a winner and we all worked on our roles to do that."

Though they held a 3–1 lead heading back to Vancouver, the Canucks weren't able to close the door on Marian Gaborik and the Minnesota Wild, who won the series in seven games.

16 MONTREAL CANADIENS – 1992-93

THE IDEA OF THE LEAGUE'S most decorated franchise re-uniting with the Stanley Cup on the chalice's 100th anniversary seems storybook. But the 1992-93 Montreal Canadiens defied odds and re-wrote the record book on the road to their 24th championship.

Riding the spectacular play of Conn Smythe-winning goaltender Patrick Roy, the Canadiens tied the mark for most consecutive wins by one team in a playoff with 11, victimizing the Nordiques, Sabres and Islanders to punch their ticket to the final.

"I just had so much confidence in my teammates," said Roy at the time. "It's just a matter of time, I keep making saves and we'll win."

The club also set a record of 10 playoff overtime wins in one year – a feat that may never be touched.

Thanks in big part to the heroics of goalie Patrick Roy, the Canadiens racked up 10 overtime wins in the 1993 playoffs and upended the Kings in the final.

The team was not a juggernaut; it finished third in the Adams Division and seventh overall during the regular season with 102 points. But it had impressive depth and clutch performers with the capacity to excel when it mattered most. The group included Vincent Damphousse, Kirk Muller, Brian Bellows and 23-year-old John LeClair up front. Add that to a young blueline, including Mathieu Schneider, Eric Desjardins and Patrice Brisebois, and an acute game plan engineered by coach Jacques Demers, and it was a date with destiny.

The story's final chapter had the Canadiens matched up against the antagonist, Wayne Gretzky and his Los Angeles Kings.

Spotting the Kings Game 1, the Habs salvaged three overtime wins – with LeClair netting two game-winners – to put a head-lock on the series. But before LeClair's Game 4 heroics, Roy made the bold statement that he was only letting in two goals. They ended up winning 3-2.

Captain Guy Carbonneau shadowed 'The Great One' all series and kept him shotless in Game 5, raising another banner to the rafters.

"It's a dream, it's a dream," Schneider said after the win. "Pinch me, wake me up, somebody."

17 NASHVILLE PREDATORS – 2006-07

IN RETROSPECT, it was a historically jarring moment for a star-crossed franchise. The 2006-07 Nashville Predators, small-market sellers for most of their existence, landed the biggest name available at the NHL trade deadline.

Peter Forsberg, 'Foppa' to his admirers, came to Music City in a blockbuster deal that sent left winger Scottie Upshall, defenseman Ryan Parent, plus the Preds' first and third round selections in the 2007 draft to Philadelphia.

The move sent a bold message to a group of players in the midst of putting together Nashville's best year to date, a campaign that would see the Preds rack up 110 points in the regular season.

J-P Dumont and Peter Forsberg helped the Nashville Predators put up 110 points in the 2006–07 regular season, but couldn't get them past the San Jose Sharks in the opening round of the playoffs.

"He was one of the best players of the 1990s," said David Legwand, the first draft pick in Predators history. "It was awesome to have him and learn from him."

The Preds finished second in points in the Western Conference, but were unfortunately behind division rival Detroit, thus relegating Nashville to the fourth seed in the playoffs and a date with the potent San Jose Sharks, who dispatched them in five games. For a team used to losing assets due to financial constraints, the Preds marched out an impressive roster in '06-07 that featured Paul Kariya, Jason Arnott, Tomas Vokoun, Kimmo Timonen, Alexander Radulov and Steve Sullivan, whose season was cut short by a major back injury.

"That was the most talented team we've had," said Barry Trotz, the team's first coach. "They were a good group and they believed they could win the Cup and that was the first time we believed we could. The downside was that we never got to see that because we had a lot of people out with injuries come playoff time.

"If we could've stayed healthy, I would've liked to see if we could've done some damage."

18 NEW JERSEY DEVILS – 2002-03

The 2002-03 New Jersey Devils were comprised of multiple future Hall of Fame players nearing crossroads in their NHL careers. So it was no wonder they played virtually every game like there was no tomorrow and won the third Stanley Cup in franchise history.

The Devils rampaged through the regular season, finishing first in the Atlantic Division and second in the Eastern Conference thanks to yeoman's work by the usual suspects – left winger Patrik Elias, defensemen Scott Niedermayer and Scott Stevens, and goalie Martin Brodeur.

After relatively easy wins in their first two playoff series against Boston and Tampa Bay, the Devils faced a real test in the Eastern Conference final against the Ottawa Senators, who won the Presidents' Trophy that year as the NHL's best regular-season team.

They beat the seemingly superior Sens in seven hotly contested games, including a final showdown not decided until Jeff Friesen scored with three minutes remaining in regulation.

From there, the Devils took on the Mighty Ducks of Anaheim, first-time Cup finalists led by star Paul Kariya and netminder Jean-Sebastien Giguere.

For the first time since 1965, the home team won every game in the Cup final. Luckily for the Devils, they had home ice advantage.

Goaltender Martin Brodeur's 2003 Cup is one of three he's won during his time with the New Jersey Devils.

And although Giguere won the Conn Smythe Trophy as playoff MVP, it was the efforts of Brodeur (1.65 goals-against average and .934 save percentage in 24 playoff games), Niedermayer (a team-best 16 assists and 18 points) and Stevens (who knocked Kariya unconscious in Game 6) that gave the Devils the Cup.

"I never would have thought this would have happened again," Stevens said at the time. "We started the year and built and worked hard as a team and we've got a lot of character guys... Once again we found a way to win the last game of the year."

Less than two years later, Stevens retired and Niedermayer moved on to Anaheim as a free agent.

And the Devils have failed to make the Cup final ever since.

19 NEW YORK ISLANDERS – 1992-93

WHEN YOU THINK of great New York Islanders teams, you don't get past the mid-1980s. But in 1993, a team from the Isle shocked the two-time defending Stanley Cup champion Pittsburgh Penguins en route to the Wales Conference final.

After dispatching the Capitals in Round 1, the Islanders met the Presidents' Trophy-winning Pens, who finished 32 points ahead of New York. And they did so without Pierre Turgeon (58 goals, 132 points), who was felled by a Dale Hunter cheap shot after scoring the series-deciding goal against Washington.

Pittsburgh, meanwhile, boasted a murderer's row that included Mario Lemieux (69 goals and 160 points in 60 games); Kevin Stevens, Rick Tocchet and Ron Francis, all 100-plus-point producers; a 20-year-old Jaromir Jagr (94 points); defenseman Larry Murphy (22 goals and 85 points); and second-team all-star Tom Barrasso in goal.

When the series began, Islanders coach Al Arbour simply asked every player if they could tie a shift against Lemieux – not score, not even win, just tie.

Ray Ferraro led the Islanders in playoff scoring with 13 goals and 20 points in 18 games in 1992–93.

"And then when we got to the 12th or 13th man he said, 'Good. There's the first period,' " Islanders starting goaltender Glenn Healy remembered. "And then he started all over again."

New York forechecked and frustrated Pittsburgh for five games and won the sixth 7-5 to force Game 7. That final game looked to be in the bag with a few minutes to play, New York up 3-1 and Lemieux in the penalty box.

"I can remember thinking 'Ah f---, here we go! (Lemieux) is off for two minutes, we won!' " Healy said. "And they scored two goals in, like, 20 seconds."

With the momentum squarely in the Penguins' favor, New York's fortunes looked bleak. That is until winger David Volek scored 5:16 into overtime, sending the mighty Penguins packing and the Islanders to the conference final against the eventual Cup champion Montreal Canadiens.

"We should have won the Cup," Murphy said of the Pens' season. "To this day, that was the toughest loss of my career."

20 NEW YORK RANGERS – 1971-72

DESPITE LOSING THE STANLEY CUP FINAL, for the 1971-72 New York Rangers, 'GAG' was a positive term.

The 'GAG line' (Goal-A-Game) was the nickname given to the dominant Rangers' trio of Jean Ratelle, Vic Hadfield and Rod Gilbert, who were 1-2-3 in team scoring and 3-4-5 in the league during the regular season.

Hall of Famer Brad Park was a first team all-star and the runner up for the Norris Trophy in 1971–72.

"The GAG line was the top-ish line," said Hall of Fame defenseman Brad Park, who starred for the Rangers that season, "but I think what people don't appreciate was the second line we had with Walter Tkaczuk, Bill Fairbairn and (later) Steve Vickers. Tkaczuk and Fairburn…not only were they a powerful pair, but they also were unbelievable penalty killers."

Benefiting from two solid lines up front, a strong goaltending tandem of Ed Giacomin and Gilles Villemure, and the superb coaching of Emile Francis, the Rangers finished second in the East Division with a 48-17-13 record and qualified for their sixth consecutive post-season.

"Being coached by Emile Francis was tremendous," said Gilbert, another Hall of Famer. "The most difficult thing for a coach is to find a combination of guys that will complement each other and Emile Francis had the ability to do that…that made the difference on our team."

The Rangers took a hard hit when they lost high-scoring center Ratelle, who was on pace to become the first Ranger in 30 years to lead the NHL in scoring, 17 games before the end of the regular season. Ratelle returned for just six playoff games.

"It was crazy," said Gilbert, who finished the season with 43 goals and 97 points. "He was the most valuable player on our team, no question. If he didn't get hurt, we would have won the Stanley Cup, for sure."

Despite the loss of Ratelle, New York advanced past Montreal and Chicago before bowing out in six games in the Cup final to a great Boston team that featured Art Ross Trophy winner Phil Esposito and Norris and Hart Trophy winner Bobby Orr.

The 1971-72 Rangers didn't win the Cup, but were the most successful Blueshirts squad in 22 years and the best Broadway could boast of until the Cup-winning team of 1994.

21 OTTAWA SENATORS – 2006-07

AFTER YEARS of talented squads that underachieved in the playoffs, the Ottawa Senators finally broke through in 2006-07, riding a glut of scoring all the way to the Stanley Cup final.

"Our roles were really specified on that team," said defenseman Joe Corvo. "We had our scoring line that we depended heavily on and thereafter everybody did their job to a 'T'."

That scoring line was the dynamic trio of center Jason Spezza between wingers Daniel Alfredsson and Dany Heatley. In the

Mike Fisher, with 10 points, finished tied for second and Daniel Alfredsson, with 22, tied for first in team scoring during the 2007 playoffs for the Senators.

regular season, Heatley was fourth in NHL scoring with 105 points, while Spezza and Alfredsson each racked up 87. The Sens scored 286 goals in total, second only to the Buffalo Sabres (298 goals), the team Ottawa knocked out in the Eastern Conference final. But for the Senators, the run started in the second half of the regular season.

"Everything becomes automatic," Corvo recalled. "Guys are playing the same way every game and you know they're going to bring that effort. It turned into a well-oiled machine and we took that momentum into the playoffs."

With Ray Emery holding down the fort in net, the Sens once again turned to their big line up front. Spezza, Heatley and Alfredsson led the NHL in post-season scoring with remarkable synchronicity: each player tallied 22 points in 20 games. The team lost just once per series in matchups against Sidney Crosby's Penguins, Martin Brodeur's Devils and the loaded Sabres squad featuring Daniel Briere, Chris Drury, Thomas Vanek and burgeoning star netminder Ryan Miller.

But in the Stanley Cup final, Ottawa faced the big, bad Anaheim Ducks. Led by behemoth defenseman Chris Pronger, the Ducks outmuscled Ottawa, dispatching the Sens in five games.

"They bullied us around," Corvo said. "That was their game plan. If you watched any film on us you'd know we weren't the biggest hitting team or the most physical team. They played their game plan well and frustrated us."

22 PHILADELPHIA FLYERS – 1979-80

THIRTY-FIVE GAMES. Three months. No losses.

The 1979-80 Flyers lost their second game of the season in early October and didn't lose again until Jan. 7.

The undefeated record – 25-0-10 – still remains the standard for all North American professional teams.

Reasons for the success? First, a good mixture of aging Hall of Famers (Bobby Clarke, Bill Barber); a wave of hungry new kids

(Ken Linseman, Mel Bridgman, Behn Wilson); and a bunch of helpful plumbers (Frank Bathe, Norm Barnes, John Paddock, Mike Busniuk and Dennis Ververgaert) found its groove early.

Plus, rookie goaltender Pete Peeters and veteran Phil Myre were a perfect fit for each other.

"It was a great mix," Barber said. "We had a blend of the older and younger guys.

"The younger guys paid attention to listening and learning about what it took to win. We got great goaltending from Peeters. And when you're able to use your farm system and the minor leagues; that was an important factor for us that year, from Barnes to Bathe to Terry Murray. Those players paid off for us."

Coach Pat Quinn had his team playing the correct fashion. It would finish with a league-high 116 points (48-12-20) and take the New York Islanders to six games before falling in the Stanley Cup final.

"You talk about team play, playing the game the right way," Barber said. "There weren't any games that we were out of and not many teams can say that.

"To not lose in 35 games, it was pretty special. I find it hard to believe that it will ever be done again. That's almost half the season. We went to Atlanta in the second game of the season and got absolutely killed (9-2). From that point on we didn't lose until January."

Ken 'The Rat' Linseman was one of several youngsters on the Flyers who helped propel the team to a 35-game unbeaten streak.

23 PHOENIX COYOTES – 2009-10

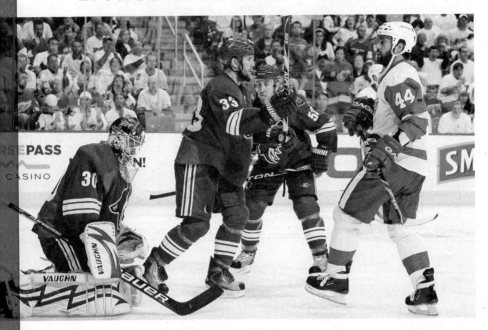

Goalie Ilya Bryzgalov and the Phoenix Coyotes put up a valiant fight against the Red Wings, but ended up losing in Game 7 of the 2010 opening round.

NAMING A BEST-EVER PHOENIX COYOTES TEAM is a little like identifying your favorite shade of beige. None truly stands out for a franchise that hasn't won a playoff round since relocating from Winnipeg before the 1996-97 season.

The nod goes to the 2009-10 edition, one which overcame a file for bankruptcy, a legal tug of war between Jim Balsillie and the NHL, questions about relocation and Wayne Gretzky's departure to post a record-breaking regular season.

Because of the litigation and uncertainty surrounding the club's future, adding high-priced free agents in the off-season wasn't an option. However, GM Don Maloney adeptly opted to shelve the youth movement and instead cobbled together a collection of veterans hungry to prove themselves. The result was a franchise-high 107-point campaign, despite prognostications of a last-place finish in the West by The Hockey News in the pre-season.

"To go from off-ice turmoil to put the focus back on the ice and on the game itself, I think we've come a long way this year," coach Dave Tippett said. "What happens now is we've set the bar higher for ourselves moving forward and it's going to be a challenge to make sure that bar goes up again."

Keys to success were goalie Ilya Bryzgalov, whose brilliance earned him a Vezina Trophy nomination, and Tippett, whose bench mastery put him in the running for the Jack Adams Award.

Without an elite scoring presence – the Coyotes didn't have any player among the league's top 40 point-getters – it was all about team play and adherence to systems.

Sadly for Yotes supporters, the team bowed out yet again in Round 1, this time in seven games to the powerful Detroit Red Wings. But their dramatic run to the playoffs set the tone for a brighter future.

"If someone would have told us in training camp we'd finish with 107 points, 50 wins, we would have probably told them they were crazy," said center Vernon Fiddler. "We took a great team to Game 7, where anything can happen, and they just played better than us in one of the games."

24 PITTSBURGH PENGUINS – 1992-93

THEY WERE A STEAMROLLER stopped by a field mouse.

The 1992-93 Pittsburgh Penguins were machine-like in their power and precision, a club everyone expected to win its third consecutive Stanley Cup. To review:

• Their 119 points were most in franchise history, earning them their first and only Presidents' Trophy as regular season champs.

• Their 367 goals for were their best ever; so, too, was their plus-99 goal differential.

• They set an NHL record with 17 consecutive wins down the stretch.

• Their captain, Mario Lemieux, had one of the greatest individual campaigns hockey has ever known. Despite missing 24 games while being treated for Hodgkin's disease, he returned to win the scoring title by 12 points. In addition to the Art Ross, Lemieux won the Hart Trophy as NHL MVP, the Masterton for

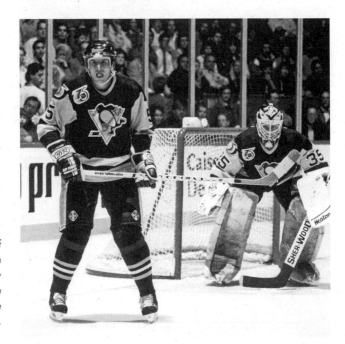

Blueliner Ulf Samuelsson set a career high for penalty minutes with 249 on the 1992–93 edition of the Penguins.

perseverance and dedication, the Pearson as his peer's pick as best player and was named the first-team all-star center.

• Goalie Tom Barrasso, left winger Kevin Stevens and defenseman Larry Murphy each earned second-team all-star nods.

• Four Pens – Lemieux, Stevens, Rick Tocchet and Ron Francis – had 100 or more points. Stevens connected on 55 goals, Tocchet 48.

Add in future Hall-of-Famers Jaromir Jagr and Joe Mullen and legendary coach Scotty Bowman, and it's a no-brainer to crown this group the greatest collection in franchise history (Cup years notwithstanding).

That's what made their second round playoff setback to the New York Islanders – a team that squeaked into the post-season and one missing its best player in Pierre Turgeon – so crushing.

"(It was) my most disappointing season… disappointing team-wise," Murphy remembers. "We should have won the Cup. To this day, that was the toughest loss of my career."

The Isles won the Patrick Division final in seven games, when winger David Volek, an eight-goal scorer during the season, beat Barrasso with a slap shot in overtime. With the Isles finishing 32 points behind Pittsburgh in the regular season, the upset is considered one of the most shocking in league annals.

25 SAN JOSE SHARKS – 2003-04

THE SAN JOSE SHARKS franchise has been teetering on the edge of glory for many years now. A perennial regular season powerhouse, the team has experienced only minimal playoff success.

The 2003-04 version of the teal and black may not have been loaded with stars and offensive power, but they were young and they gelled at the right time.

It was a season that saw the emergence of a new generation in San Jose. The team was led in goal scoring by 24-year-old Patrick Marleau and 23-year-old Jonathan Cheechoo. Both players found the net 28 times and Marleau led the Sharks in points with 57. A 25-year-old Marco Sturm also had a productive season, netting 21 goals and 41 points. Brad Stuart, 24, led the rearguards, posting a career-high 39 points.

The Sharks believed in their youth movement so much that they dealt long-time Shark captain Nolan to the Toronto Maple Leafs for Alyn McCauley, Brad Boyes and a first round pick that later

The Sharks found their bite in the 2004 post-season, reaching the conference final for the first time.

became Mark Stuart. This was a move that further solidified management's commitment to retool.

Depth between the pipes was a non-issue. The Sharks had Evgeni Nabokov starting and a solid backup in Vesa Toskala. Waiting in the midst was a young Finn by the name of Miikka Kiprusoff.

Coming off a season where they didn't even qualify for the play-offs, the Sharks claimed the Pacific Division title and got past the St. Louis Blues and Colorado Avalanche in the first two post-season rounds with only three losses. However, they ran in to a determined Calgary Flames team led by Jarome Iginla and were ousted in the Western Conference final, 4-2.

While the Sharks have yet to sink their teeth into the Stanley Cup, the '03-04 youth movement provided fans with their deepest dive into the playoffs.

"It's a huge step for the whole organization," said Nabokov at the time.

26 ST. LOUIS BLUES – 1968-69

THE ST. LOUIS BLUES were still new to the NHL in 1968-69, but their roster oozed experience.

Led by legendary defenseman Doug Harvey, 44, the Blues had six players older than coach Scotty Bowman, who was 35 at the time.

Left winger Red Berenson said it was that wisdom of Harvey, along with other veterans including 40-year-old Jacques Plante, 36-year-olds Jean-Guy Talbot, Al Arbour and Glenn Hall and 35-year-old Camille Henry, that guided the second-year Blues to their second straight Stanley Cup final appearance.

"There was a lot of respect," remembers Berenson, who led the team with 35 goals and 82 points in the best offensive season of his career. "And those players weren't just old players. They were players who had played for Stanley Cup teams, particu-larly Montreal. If you look at most of the players that were older, it was players that Scotty had hand picked himself to play for St. Louis because he knew they were winners and they knew how to win. That was big factor."

The Blues finished atop the Western Division with a 37-25-14 record. They were also the best defensive team in the league by a long shot, allowing just 157 goals – 39 fewer than second best.

The defensive success was thanks to the Hall of Fame goaltending duo of Hall and Plante and a steady blueline patrolled by Harvey and Arbour.

"They were as good as it gets," said Berenson, the University of Michigan's coach since 1984. "We didn't have to score a lot of goals to win a game."

The Blues cruised to the Stanley Cup final without losing a game, sweeping Philadelphia and Los Angeles, but were swept themselves by the Montreal Canadiens for the second straight year.

"We had a pretty good season," Bowman said at the time. "Won the Western division, won the playoffs in the West, won the Vezina Trophy, had a player (Red Berenson) score six goals in one game to tie an all-time record. Not a bad season."

27 TAMPA BAY LIGHTNING – 2003-04

THE 2003-04 TAMPA BAY Lightning was riddled with storylines, ranging from a coach feuding with a star player to a key defensive acquisition. The equation may not be traditional, but the results were ideal.

The Lightning was coming off its first playoff season since 1996 and wanted to prove it was capable of more than a one-and-done scenario.

"I think we learned a lot from that season before," said Jay Feaster, Tampa's GM at the time. "I felt that after the 2002-03 season we could still show that we were going to be Southeast Division champs. The issue was: how much further could we go in the playoffs."

It wasn't long before the Lightning found out they could go all the way. After steamrolling the New York Islanders and Montreal Canadiens in the first two rounds, the Lightning went on to conquer the Philadelphia Flyers in seven, claiming its first Eastern Conference title.

On a roster chock-full of offensive talent, it was the relatively unknown Ruslan Fedotenko who scored the Game 7 game-winning goal against the Calgary Flames that brought the Stanley Cup to the state of Florida for the first time.

Despite all the star power – Martin St-Louis, Brad Richards, Vincent Lecavalier, Dan Boyle, Nikolai Khabibulin and a wily vet and rallying-point (due to his 22 seasons without a Cup) in Dave Andreychuk – Feaster believes it was the off-the-radar acquisition of defenseman Darryl Sydor prior to the trade deadline that made the difference.

"Acquiring him was huge, we had to have another experienced defenseman back there if we were going to do anything in the playoffs," Feaster said. "It was Syd who was the one talking to the team about 'how you can play your whole career and never have a shot like we have with this kind of team' and that 'this is an opportunity that you cannot let go by.' Between that and his play, if he isn't part of it, I don't know if we make that run."

Dave Andreychuk waited 22 seasons to hoist the Stanley Cup, but got his chance with the Lightning in 2004.

28 TORONTO MAPLE LEAFS – 1966-67

Ron Ellis spent his entire NHL career, spanning more than 1,000 games, with the Toronto Maple Leafs.

WHAT WAS THE BEST Maple Leafs team that didn't make THN's all-time top 25? It has to be the 1966-67 group, doesn't it?

The squad – the last Toronto outfit to win the Stanley Cup – was chock-full of veterans (including future Hall of Famers Tim Horton, George Armstrong and Red Kelly) and backstopped by legendary goalies Terry Sawchuk and Johnny Bower.

There was no shortage of talented youngsters, either. Right winger Ron Ellis, 21, scored a team-best 22 goals that season; heart-and-soul center Dave Keon, who led Toronto in points, was 26; left winger Frank Mahovlich was 28; and center Pete Stemkowski was 23.

"That team was younger than the last (Leafs) team I won (a Cup) with," said Hall of Fame left winger Dick Duff, who won back-to-back Cups with the Leafs ('63 and '64) before moving on to New York the next season. "Keon was the class of the league and Ellis gave them some real scoring power. And their goalies…Bower or Sawchuk could steal a game from you at any time."

Helmed by coach-GM Punch Imlach, the '66-67 Leafs finished third in the league during the regular season – despite losing 10 straight games mid-year – and beat the first place Chicago Black Hawks in the semifinal. The Leafs faced their archrivals from Montreal in the Cup final.

The epic series that ensued featured a standout showing from Toronto's line of Stemkowski, Jim Pappin and Bob Pulford, a Conn Smythe Trophy-winning performance from Keon and a goalie platoon (sometimes out of necessity due to injury) through the first four games.

It finished in a roller-coaster-like six games, with the Leafs winning their 11th Cup in franchise history.

"Stemkowski gave them a big boost," said Duff, who played for the Canadiens that year. "They were really balanced and they won when it counted."

29 VANCOUVER CANUCKS – 1993-94

BEING ONE OF THE 13 TEAMS in the NHL to have never won a Stanley Cup makes reminiscing about the glory days bittersweet. The 1993-94 Vancouver Canucks' run to the final was, ultimately, a footnote in the history books that weaves a tale of a New York Rangers team poised and determined to end a 54-year Cup drought.

Led by captain Trevor Linden, the Canucks started the season with a 7-1-0 run. By the all-star break, however, the Canucks had slipped to .500, despite Linden's team-leading 24 goals. Linden wilted in the second half of the season, managing just eight goals in his final 39 games. Fortunately for the Canucks, they entered the playoffs with another offensive gem: Pavel Bure.

After an average first half, Bure scored 40 goals in his final 42 games, reaching the 60-goal plateau for a second-consecutive season. The Russian Rocket contributed a team-leading 16-playoff goals, helping the club reach the final.

Naturally, there were other key performers for the seventh-seeded Canucks. Goalie Kirk McLean, viewed by some as a weakness entering the post-season, silenced his critics in the first round against Calgary with what was called, simply, "The Save."

In Game 7, McLean came up huge in overtime, stoning Robert Reichel with a desperate cross-crease pad stop before Bure's winner in the second extra frame. The Canucks rode the emotion of the Calgary series into five-game dispatches of the Dallas Stars and the Toronto Maple Leafs in the semis and conference final. For the second time in franchise history, the Canucks had made it to the Cup final.

Facing a Rangers team led by Mark Messier, the Canucks forced a Game 7, but even a two-goal performance by Linden wasn't enough to thrust the team to Stanley Cup glory and the Rangers won the game 3-2.

"What makes this extra special was that Vancouver was such a great opponent," said Messier at the time, offering the most bittersweet of compliments.

Kirk McLean is famous in Vancouver – and Calgary – for "The Save" during the 1994 playoffs.

30 WASHINGTON CAPITALS – 1997-98

THE 1997-98 WASHINGTON CAPITALS were no regular season juggernaut, but they bled character, which proved to be a catalyst for an unlikely run to the Stanley Cup final.

The Capitals boasted the league's top penalty kill and the highest winning percentage after trailing in the first period, showcasing their heart and a desire to compete.

With captain Dale Hunter, who sits second all-time in NHL penalty minutes, and a new pragmatic bench boss in Ron Wilson, the team had a solid backbone.

Up front, they were propelled by franchise points leader Peter Bondra, who netted 52 goals that season, along with skilled pivots Adam Oates and Joe Juneau. On the back end, which featured dependable Calle Johansson and free-wheeling Phil Housley, the Caps were effective.

The team also had ripening stars Andrew Brunette and Sergei Gonchar, not to mention standout goaltender Olaf Kolzig. 'Olie the Goalie' posted a 2.20 goals-against average and .920 save percentage, padding his franchise lead in wins and shutouts.

Fueled by a 6-2-1 record down the stretch, the Capitals finished fourth in the East and watched the top three seeds, New Jersey, Philadelphia and Pittsburgh, get upended in the first round, clearing the way for the Caps to leverage home ice the rest of the way. They did their part by knocking off Boston, Ottawa and Buffalo, winning six overtime games in the process.

"We all felt, myself included, that it was destiny," Kolzig said. "With everything that was going on, the right teams were falling by the wayside."

Facing off against a dynasty in Detroit, the Caps championship dreams came to a sudden halt. The Wings swept the series to capture their second consecutive Stanley Cup.

"You're just as disappointed as a team who doesn't make the playoffs because you didn't win the Cup," Kolzig said. "But nobody expected us or had any expectations of us to go to the final and lose to Detroit. We kind of hang our hat on that."

Olaf Kolzig's 1.95 GAA and .944 SP in the playoffs helped the Capitals reach the 1998 final before falling short against the Red Wings.

PHOTO CREDITS

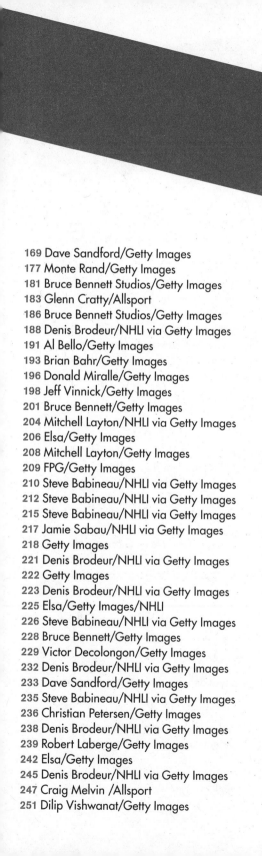

ACKNOWLEDGEMENTS

Pulling together The Greatest Hockey Teams of All-Time needed an all-time effort from all involved and from top to bottom everyone came up with a performance for the ages.

The Hockey News editor in chief, Jason Kay, for keeping the team in line and motivated throughout. Edward Fraser, the magazine's managing editor, for directing traffic and ensuring all aspects received the treatment they deserved.

Sam McCaig for getting the ball rolling and doing much of the heavy lifting early on.

The THN staff – Rory Boylen, Ken Campbell, Ryan Dixon, John Grigg, Ryan Kennedy, Adam Proteau – and the interns – Nikki Cook, Hilary Hagerman, Kevin Hall, Brandon Macdonald, Corey Johnson, Kyle Palantzas, Dustin Pollack, Jamie Ross, Nick Spector – for their tireless writing, editing and fact-checking.

Freelancers Jim Cressman, Wayne Fish, Denis Gibbons, Mike Heika, Neil Hodge, Mike Mastovich, Kevin Oklobzija, James Shewaga, Ronnie Shuker and Rob Rossi for their expertise and for filling the voids.

Hockey historians Ernie Fitzsimmons and Kevin Shea and all the other players, coaches, GMs and media-types for taking the time to talk to us.

Art Director Jamie Hodgson and designer Erika Vanderveer for arranging the art.

The management team of THN publisher Caroline Andrews and book publisher Jean Pare for their work behind the scenes.

And to the members of the marketing/communications department, Janis Davidson-Pressick, Carlie McGhee and Alyson Young, for helping to get the word out.